TEACHING THINKING SKILLS
WITH FAIRY TALES AND FANTASY

TEACHING THINKING SKILLS
WITH FAIRY TALES AND FANTASY

Nancy Polette

Teacher Ideas Press, an imprint of Libraries Unlimited
Westport, Connecticut · London

Library of Congress Cataloging-in-Publication Data

Polette, Nancy.
    Teaching thinking skills with fairy tales and fantasy / by Nancy Polette.
      p. cm
    Includes bibliographical references and index.
    ISBN 1-59158-320-9 (pbk. : alk. paper)
    1. Thought and thinking—Study and teaching. 2. Fairy tales—Study and teaching.
  I. Title.
  LB1590.3.T653   2005
  370.15'2—dc22   2005016097

British Library Cataloguing in Publication Date is available.

Library of Congress Catalog Card Number: 2005016097
ISBN: 1-59158-320-9

First published in 2005

Teacher Ideas Press/Libraries Unlimited, 88 Post Road West, Westport, CT 06881
A Member of Greenwood Publishing Group, Inc.
www.lu.com

Printed in the United States of America

The paper used in this book complies with the
Permanent Paper Standard issued by the National
Information Standards Organization (Z39.48–1984).

10 9 8 7 6 5 4 3 2 1

CONTENTS

INTRODUCTION

Fairy tales and fantasy do help to shape great minds. Einstein was an avid reader of fairy tales. Understanding real humanity, nobility of character, and the vitality of love through traditional tales rather than through counterfeit, superficial, remote, and plastic mannikins of the media world, helps one to live life deeply.

Students need to be given the opportunity through fairy tales and fantasy to develop an elasticity of mind. Many dragons face us all in life today, and fortunate is the child who has tilted with many on his path and emerged victorious. Fortunate, too, is the child who has won dragons to his side through gentleness and understanding. The child will need both skills in the years ahead. What better skill sharpener than exposure to meaningful stories that have withstood the test of time?

Our schools have tended to overemphasize the steam shovel approach to learning. The how-to first book of atoms, magnets, automobiles, and pumpkin pies abound in classrooms and school libraries. In teaching the anatomy of a bird's wings, we must not allow children to lose the awe of flight.

Teaching Thinking Skills with Fairy Tales and Fantasy is an easy-to-use guide to teaching those skills that have been identified as needing practice by students in grades one through six. Each skill is defined and explained on a large-print page, which can be used as a transparency master.

The introduction of a skill is followed by one or more activities using familiar fairy tale and fantasy characters, settings, and plots as a springboard to learning the skill. Each activity is complete and needs no other materials to use. However, it is hoped that students will be motivated to read those tales with which they are not familiar. A complete bibliography of titles mentioned is included.

All skills introduced can be immediately applied to other areas of the curriculum as well as to real life situations. Here is a painless approach to helping students become better thinkers by exercising skills that will also improve reading and writing ability.

1

WHAT IS THINKING?

Thinking begins with

| A question |
| A need |
| A problem |

Good thinking uses the skills of

Analysis	Hypothesizing
Association	Interpretation
Classification	Observation
Comprehension	Planning
Comparison	Predicting
Deduction	Questioning
Evaluation	Sequencing
Flexibility	Synthesizing
Fluency	Theorizing
Forecasting	AND
Generalizing	MORE!

Good thinking results in

New skills, concepts, decisions, actions, discoveries, ideas, or methods; new questions or needs.

WHO NEEDS THINKING SKILLS?

Ina **Impulsive** Skills needed: Decision-making, problem-solving, analysis, forecasting	Goes with first idea regardless of consequences **Danny** **Dependent** Skills needed: Productive, inductive, and deductive thinking

Ina
Impulsive

Goes with first idea regardless of consequences

Skills needed: Decision-making, problem-solving, analysis, forecasting

Danny
Dependent

Always needs help

Skills needed: Productive, inductive, and deductive thinking

Al
Always

Goes all directions at once—never reaches goal

Skills needed: Deductive thinking, planning, analysis, problem-solving

Rita
Rigid

Uses only learned information

Skills needed: Fluency, flexibility, creativity thinking, perceptual thinking

Belinda
Believer

Believes everything written must be true

Skills needed: Critical thinking, hypothesizing, evaluating, judging

Robert
Right

1

Sticks to his idea regardless of evidence

Skills needed: Analysis, synthesis, comparing, evaluation

Fred
Fear

Never responds for fear of being wrong

Skills needed: Productive thinking, deductive thinking, problem-solving

Dora
Dense

?

Usual comment: "I don't understand."

Skills needed: Conceptualization, abstract, thinking, intepretation

ABSTRACT THINKING

Expressing a quality apart from an object displaying it

1. State the abstract concept to be developed.
   Example: Freedom

2. Give positive examples of the concept.
   These characters are free:
   Peter Pan, Mary Poppins

3. Give non-examples of the concept.
   These characters are not free:
   Hansel & Gretel in the witch's cottage

4. Examine and list only those attributes which apply solely to the concept.
   Freedom of choice, of speech

5. Define the concept.
   Not subject to the control or outside domination of another.

MAKING THE ABSTRACT CONCRETE

Personification is one way to demonstrate understanding of abstract concepts. Using personification, the concept is given human qualities.

EXAMPLE: FREEDOM

I am Freedom.

My home is wherever people have choices.

My flag is the red, white, and blue of democracy.

I wear a suit of armor in defense of liberty.

My job is to defend liberty wherever it may be threatened.

Choice and Responsibility are my cousins.

When I vacation, those who dominate are successful.

I move with sureness and the certainty that all people want me.

Give human qualities to one of these abstract concepts.

Choose from: Justice, Responsibility, Love, Courage, Fear, Anger

1. What are you? _____

2. Where do you live? _____

3. Favorite colors _____

4. Favorite clothes _____

5. What is your job? _____

6. Who are your family/friends?_____

7. What happens when you vacation? _____

8. How do you move? _____

MAKING THE ABSTRACT CONCRETE

Snow White's wicked stepmother ordered the huntsman to take the girl into the forest and kill her. The huntsman took Snow White deep into the forest, but as afternooon shadows deepened, he could not kill her. He let her go on alone. She ran over sharp stones and through thorn bushes. When **twilight** drew near she came to a little house. She went inside to rest. Everything was very small but as pretty and clean as possible. Being very tired she laid down and went to sleep.

ABSTRACT CONCEPT: TWILIGHT

I am Grandmother Twilight,

putting the sun to bed

behind towering mountain tops.

My cloak is a mantle of darkness.

In my hand I hold a lighted match

that flickers and then dies,

leaving my cousin, Night,

to celebrate the dawn,

and I vacation under the sun's warm rays.

Use this pattern to write about: Morning, Evening, Sunrise, Night, Dawn.

1. What are you? _____

2. Where do you live? _____

3. Favorite colors _____

4. Favorite clothes _____

5. What is your job? _____

6. Who are your family/friends?_____

7. Where do you vacation? _____

8. How do you move? _____

AFFECTIVE DOMAIN

RECEPTIVENESS
Willing to pay attention.
Willing to become aware.
Sensitive to human needs.

RESPONSIVENESS
Willing to participate, discuss, justify.

VALUE-DRIVEN
Placing value or worth on an object or idea.
Demonstrating beliefs.

ORGANIZATION
Formulates plans consistent with beliefs.
Brings together and examines values.
Resolves conflicts between values.
Internalizing values.

CHARACTERIZATION BY A VALUE
Develops lifestyle based on specific values.
Demonstrating self-reliance, discrimination,
verification.

AFFECTIVE DOMAIN: THE UGLY DUCKLING

Share the story poem adapted from the tale by Hans Christian Andersen

(adapted by Nancy Polette)

One summer day
a mother duck
heard her
cracking eggs.
She stepped aside
and watched emerge
ten tiny legs.
All eggs but one
had come apart.
Five baby ducks
stepped out.
And from the last, the
giant egg,
stepped an
ugly lout.
The ducks they bit,
the hens they pecked
the ugly duckling's
side,
and when the girl
gave him a kick,
he ran away
to hide.
All through summer,
all through the fall

the duckling hid
from others.
He had no home,
no place,
no friends,
no sisters, and
no brothers.
The bitter cold
of winter came.
In ice
he'd frozen fast.
A farmer
came along
and saw
the duckling
breathe his last.
He rescued him
and took him home
to his old
shrieking wife.
The duck awoke
and flew away,
fearful for
his life.
In spring he saw

the royal swans
floating on
the lake.
He swam to them
and cried aloud,
"My life is yours
to take!"
Just then below
the water's edge
emerged
the unexpected.
For in the image
mirrored there,
he saw a swan
reflected.
And from the shore
he heard the
glowing praises
of the crowd,
and hid his head,
for he
had learned
a kind heart
is not proud.

Examine the Affective Domain responses on the next page.

AFFECTIVE DOMAIN: SAMPLE QUESTIONS

Receiving: Sensitive to human needs.

Describe the feelings of the duckling before he became a swan.

Responding: Participate, discuss, justify.

Allow yourself to become the duckling at the time the other birds rejected him. How did it feel?

Valuing: Demonstrates beliefs.

Persuade your partner or your classmates that being different can be a very good thing.

Organization: Formulates a plan consistent with beliefs.

Suppose the duckling had not left the farmyard. How might he gain acceptance of the other birds?

Characterization by a value: Demonstrates self-reliance, discriminates, verifies.

Is beauty essential for success in life? Why or why not?

Exercise: After reading the fable that follows, develop a response for each step of the Affective Domain.

THE LION AND THE MOUSE

Adapted from an Aesop's Fable

One day a lion was disturbed by a mouse who tickled his nose. The lion grabbed the mouse and was ready to eat him when the mouse cried out, "Please, Sir Lion, if you let me go, perhaps some day I can help you." The lion laughed and laughed at the thought of a mouse helping him, but he let the mouse go.

Shortly thereafter the lion was caught in a hunter's net. The mouse heard the lion's loud roar and went to see what was the matter. Seeing that his big friend was caught, the mouse began to gnaw on the ropes and chewed a hole big enough for the lion to escape.

ANALYZE

To take apart, and identify elements, characteristics, or relationships.

1. Identify useful ways to break the person, item, or situation to be analyzed into parts.

2. Define each part clearly.

3. Identify and organize data related to each part.

4. State conclusion(s) based on analysis.

ANALYZING PROBLEMS IN MOTHER GOOSE LAND

Little Bo Peep has lost her sheep
And can't tell where to find them.
Leave them alone
And they will come home
Wagging their tails behind them.

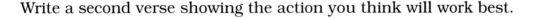

Analyze:
Is doing nothing the best way to find the sheep?
What might have caused the sheep to wander?
What do you think Bo Peep was doing when the sheep wandered away?
List other actions Bo Peep might take to find her sheep.

Write a second verse showing the action you think will work best.

EXAMPLE:

Little Bo Peep has lost her sheep
And can't tell where to find them.
If she blows a horn in the early morn
They'll come wagging their tails behind them.

EXERCISE:

Analyze each of the problems below.
How many solutions can you create?
Write a second verse showing how to solve one of the problems.

1. The sheep and the cows are running loose while Little Boy Blue sleeps.

2. The cupboard is bare in Mother Hubbard s house.

3. Three men go to sea in a leaky tub.

4. The old woman in the shoe didn't know what to do with all her children.

5. Humpty Dumpty could not be put back together again.

6. Three little kittens lost their mittens.

See: *Flying with Mother Goose* by Nancy Polette, Pieces of Learning, Marion, IL, 2003.

ANALYZING CHARACTERS

Think of a question that each of these literary characters might ask the other. Analyze the personality or characteristics of each character. Your question needs to be related in some way to the character traits of each character.

1. What directions might Prince Charming ask of Rapunzel?

2. What question might Jack (of "Jack and the Beanstalk") ask of Paul Bunyan?

3. What would Cinderella ask to borrow from Rumplestiltskin?

4. What question might Snow White ask Sleeping Beauty?

5. If Henny Penny were to pass by the troll under the bridge in "The Three Billy Goats Gruff," what would she ask?

6. What question would the wolf in "Red Riding Hood" have for the wolf in "The Three Little Pigs"?

7. What question might the witch in "Snow White" ask the witch in the gingerbread house in "Hansel and Gretel"?

8. What question might Tom Thumb have for the giant in "Jack and the Beanstalk"?

9. What question might the Twelve Dancing Princesses ask the shoemaker from "The Elves and the Shoemaker"?

10. What would Goldilocks ask to borrow from Little Red Riding Hood? Why?

ASSOCIATIVE THINKING

1. Identify basic attributes of the first item, event, or group.

2. Identify basic attributes of additional items, events, or groups.

3. Identify those attributes similar to both items, events, and groups.

Complete the following statement:

_____

is like_____

because_____

_____

_____

AN ASSOCIATIVE THINKING GAME

BOOKTALK

Lon Po Po: A Red Riding Hood Story From China.
Translated and illustrated by Ed Young, Philomel, 1989

Long, long ago, a good woman lived contentedly with her three daughters, Shang, Tao, and Paotze, in the countryside of northern China. But one day she had to leave to visit their granny, so she warned the children to close the door tightly and to latch it.

Soon after, to their surprise, there was a knock at the door and a voice saying it was their granny, their Po Po. What could the children do but let her in? But what a low voice she had, what thorny hands, and what a hairy face! To discover how three little girls outwit a wicked, wicked wolf, read *Lon Po Po.*

Play the Mystery Word Game

Here are some clues that are important to the story, *Lon Po Po.* To play the game:

1. One person is the clue caller. That person asks for a volunteer to give a number between one and five. The clue caller then reads the word for the number given.

2. If the volunteer cannot guess the thing that the word describes, the clue caller asks for another volunteer to give a different number and reads the clue for that number. The game continues until a correct guess is made or all numbers are used.

ROUND ONE	ROUND TWO	ROUND THREE	ROUND FOUR
1. tall	1. round	1. soft	1. fur
2. leaves	2. woven	2. tender	2. claws
3. branches	3. empty	3. grow	3. teeth
4. bark	4. handle	4. tree	4. thorny
5. nuts (Gingko Tree)	5. large (basket)	5. magic (Gingko Nuts)	5. hairy (wolf)

14

ASSOCIATIVE THINKING

By finding common elements between words and objects, riddle-makers become good associative thinkers.

Create beanstalk riddles.

Step One:

List words that rhyme with *bean:*

clean, mean, lean

Step Two:

Ask a question:

What would you call an angry beanstalk? A meanstalk.

What would you call a freshly scrubbed beanstalk? A cleanstalk

What would you call a skinny beanstalk? A leanstalk.

THE FOX AND THE GOAT

A fox spied a small rabbit and chased it across the meadow. The fox was so busy watching his prey that it slipped on a wet stone and fell into a deep well.

A passing goat heard the splash and leaned over to see. "Come in," said the fox. "The water is deliciously cool."

Without a thought the goat jumped into the well. "The sides are slippery," said the goat. "How will we get out?

"Let me climb up your horns and then I will pull you out," replied the fox.

"Good idea," said the goat.

So the fox climbed out and ran away.

Create Goat Riddles: List words that sound like *goat.* (*boat*)

Ask a question: What would you call a goat who likes to sail? A boat goat.

Your turn: _____

_____

_____

ASSOCIATIVE THINKING: A FAIRY TALE ALPHABET

A is for Captain Hook because he was chased by an **alligator**.

B is for Jack because he climbed a **beanstalk**.

C is for Sleeping Beauty because she went to sleep in a **castle**.

D is for the Emperor because he was **deceived** about his new clothes.

E is for Cinderella because she had to work hard **every day**.

F is for Puss-in-Boots because he helped his master make a **fortune**.

G is for the Beast because he **growled** at Beauty.

H is for the Little Match Girl because she suffered great **hardship**.

COMPLETE THESE!

I is for Jack because he was so lazy or I_____.

J is for Snow White's stepmother because she was J_____of Snow White.

K is for Mary Poppins because she was a very K_____person.

L is for the fisherman's wife because she wanted to live in L_____.

M is for the three bears because their porridge was M_____.

N is for the Frog Prince because he did not have a N_____.

O is for Jack Sprat's wife because she liked to O_____.

P is for Rapunzel who married a prince and became a P_____.

Q is for a king's wife, who is a Q_____.

R is for the Bridegroom who was really a R_____.

HOW MANY MORE CAN YOU ADD FROM S TO Z?

Key: I=idle, J=jealous, K=kind, L=luxury, M=missing, N=name, O=overeat, P=princess, Q=queen, R=robber. Other answers that can be justified are acceptable.

16

ASSOCIATIVE THINKING

The Reptile Room by Lemony Snicket, HarperCollins, 1999.

The three orphaned Baudelaire children are taken to the home of Dr. Montgomery Montgomery where they are to live. The doctor is a famed herpetologist, which means he collects and studies snakes. The children are greeted with a smile and coconut cake, and feel that things are taking a turn for the better. Dr. Montgomery plans to take them with him on his scientific expedition to Peru. However, his new assistant, Stephano, turns out to be Count Olaf, the enemy of the children. He murders Dr. Montgomery and plans to kidnap the children and take them to Peru where they won't be found. Fortunately the plucky children outwit the Count, but they are still left with no home and no family.

ASSOCIATIVE THINKING ACTIVITY

The children have to stretch their minds to come up with a plan to defeat Count Olaf. Here is a mind-stretching exercise for you to try. Name more than one thing that is ...

1.   As sinister as Count Olaf

_____

2.   As useful as a large library

_____

3.   As rotten as an apple core

_____

4.   As awful-smelling as horseradish

_____

5.   As scary as a room full of poisonous snakes

_____

6.   As irritating as a bad cough

_____

7.   As stern as a judge

_____   _____

8.   As brave as a girl kissing a snake

_____

ATTRIBUTE LISTING

1. Select and describe the object to be examined.

2. List the physical qualities (attributes) of the object.

3. List special qualities or attributes.

4. List the psychological qualities or attributes, if applicable.

5. List other objects or situations having the same qualities or attributes.

6. Combine attributes of different objects to create a new object, product, or solution.

ATTRIBUTE LISTING

A means of analyzing and separating data by observing and identifying various qualities of a particular object, character, topic, or problem.

Create a chant.

List the qualities or attributes of a giant. Use items from your list in a giant chant.

Facts About Giants

Large hands
Large feet
Large body
Large head
Loud voice
Big steps
These are just a few

Eats a lot
Steals harps
Steals hens
Roars loudly
Chases Jack
Chops beanstalks
Hoards gold, too

From near and far
Here they are
Facts about giants

List the attributes of a fairy tale hero. Write a chant.

_____   _____
_____   _____
_____   _____
_____   _____
_____   _____
_____   _____
These are just a few   _____ too.

                                  Stand and shout
                                  Bring them out
                                  Facts about_____

19

ATTRIBUTE LISTING: THE DATA BANK

BOOKTALK

Wombat Stew by Marcia Vaughan, Silver Burdette, 1986.

One day a dingo catches a furry wombat and decides to make a wombat stew. Along comes a duck-billed platypus who suggests that the stew would taste better if dingo added globs of mud. The emu arrives and wants to add feathers. Lizard wants flies added to the stew. Then echidna arrives and says no stew would be worth eating unless it had lots and lots of bugs. Finally the stew is ready. Dingo is about to toss the wombat into the pot when the other animals tell him to stop ... he has forgotten the most important thing. What do you suppose dingo has forgotten? Will wombat really end up in the stew?

Attributes of a Wombat

Lives	*Eats*	*What It Does*
Australia	roots	carries its young in a
in a burrow	vegetables	pouch
	leaves	makes an affectionate
		pet
What It Has	*Looks Like*	digs large earth
a pouch	2–3 feet long	burrows
tough hide	yellow/black color	comes out only at
long fur	furry possum	night
sharp claws		
small ears		**The Data Bank**
whiskers		

Song Pattern. Sing to the tune of "London Bridge"
(Write another verse using information from the data bank above)

Wombats eat both *roots and leaves*

Roots and leaves

Roots and leaves

Wombats *come out just at night*

And *dig burrows.*

ATTRIBUTE LISTING

In *Jack and the Beanstalk*, Jack traded the cow for some beans. Decide whether or not this was a good trade.

1. What physical characteristics do you notice about the cow?

2. What qualities make the cow a good or bad animal to have around?

3. Would it cost more to keep a cow, a hen, or a dog?

4. What benefits can a cow provide?

5. Name another animal that would be a good animal to have around for the same reasons.

6. Is a cow worth more or less than a handful of beans?

Choose a non-human fairy tale character (elf, troll, dragon, etc.). Answer the following questions.

1. What physical characteristics do you notice about the _____?

2. What qualities make the _____ a good or bad character to have around?

3. How much would it cost to keep a _____?

4. What benefits can a _____ provide?

5. Name another non-human fairy tale character that would be a good character to have around for the same reasons.

21

BRAINSTORMING

The goal of brainstorming is to produce many responses.

1. Accept all responses.

2. Withhold praise or judgment of any single response given.

3. Provide an accepting atmosphere.

4. Responses related to the ideas of others are encouraged.

5. The aim is for quantity. Not all responses will be of high quality.

BRAINSTORMING TO WRITE POETRY

It is fun to describe characters by comparing them to things we meet and use every day. Follow these directions to describe a favorite character.

1. Brainstorm things that are found in a particular place (like a kitchen or a garden) or on an object (like a car or clothing).

oven	shirt	steering wheel	hoe
bowl	button	engine	hose
pitcher	sleeve	wheels	flower
cabinet	collar	seat	seeds
blender	hat	clutch	weed
cup	cuff	chassis	spade
teapot	scarf	brake	trowel
refrigerator	pants	engine	seeds
toaster	cloak	key	rake

2. Add to this a list of human qualities and feelings.

responsibility	laughter	jealousy	dependability
accountability	joy	believer	childhood
diligence	resourcefulness	courage	courtesy
warmth	anger	helpmate	confidence
reliablility	cheer	penury	creativity
greed	honesty	cruelty	love
common sense	charity	coward	fear
faithlessness	prosperity	hate	anxiety

3. Combine the two to describe a fairy tale or fantasy character.

Examples: Harry Potter

Who Is She?   Who Is He?

A *bowlful* of common
sense
An *oven* of warmth
A *cup* of laughter
A *pitcher* full of
practical know-how
A *cabinet* of cheer

Mary Poppins

He *steers* through life
On a *seat* of
friendliness
In a *chassis* of wonder
Clutching every
opportunity
To slam the *brakes* on
evil
Ever guarding the
key
To the *engine* of the
just.

Characters	Write your description here
Peter Pan	_____
Captain Hook	_____
Cowardly Lion	_____
Dorothy	_____
Tin Woodman	_____
Scarecrow	_____
Pinocchio	_____
Iron Giant	_____

A BRAINSTORMING SESSION

Examine each situation that follows. Choose one. Brainstorm in a group MANY possible reasons for a fantasy character's action.

Why didn't Pippi Longstocking go to school every day like other nine-year-olds?

Pippi Longstocking by Astrid Lindgren

Why didn't Mary Poppins throw her old, shapeless hat away and buy a new, attractive one?

Mary Poppins by Pamela Travers

Why didn't seven-year-old Treehorn's parents notice he was shrinking?

The Shrinking of Treehorn by Florence Pary Heide

Why didn't Egan tell his cousin to go up the mountain herself if she wanted to see whether a monster really lived there?

Kneeknock Rise by Natalie Babbitt

Why didn't Zak warn the Greeg family she was going to turn them into ducks?

The Magic Finger by Roald Dahl

Why didn t her parents believe that Matilda was a genius?

Matilda by Roald Dahl

CLASSIFY/CATEGORIZE

Organizing items or concepts by characteristics, uses, word meanings, or relationships.

1. Select a basis for grouping.

2. Examine each item to identify its features or characteristics.

3. Identify similarities and differences.

4. Place items with common features in the same category or group.

WORD CATEGORIES

Add fairy tale words to each list.

Describing words	Name Words
beautiful	(Fairy tale characters)
ugly	queen
large	princess
handsome	prince
wicked	dragon
warty	toad
little	troll
	witch

Action words	Words that tell where
sits	in the kitchen
stands	under the hill
hops	above the mountain
hides	on the chair
skips	into the water
sings	between the pages
cries	on the lilypad

Use words from your word bank pages to write sentences about a character from a fairy tale.

Example: A warty toad hops into the water.

A large dragon hides under the hill.

A beautiful queen sits on the chair.

Write your sentences here:

_____

_____

_____

_____

May be copied for classroom use. *Teaching Skills with Fairy Tales and Fantasy,* by Nancy Polette
(Westport, CT: Teacher Ideas Press, an imprint of Libraries Unlimited). © 2005.

CLASSIFY/CATEGORIZE

The Seven Chinese Brothers

by Margaret Mahy

Here are vocabulary words found in the story. Put a 1 in front of each word that is a *person*. Put a 2 in front of each word that is a *place*. Put a 3 in front of each word that is a *thing*. Guess if you do not know! Read the booktalk to support or disprove guesses.

___ Ch'in Shih Huang   ___ wall

___ emperor   ___ mountains

___ China   ___ bones

___ brother   ___ iron

___ fly   ___ legs

___ miles   ___ fires

___ teardrop   ___ village

The Seven Chinese Brothers
By Margaret Mahy
Illustrated by Jean and Mou-sien Tseng
Scholastic, 1990

Once upon a time when Ch'in Shih Huang was emperor of all China, there lived seven brothers. While no one knows how it came about, each brother possessed an amazing power all his own. First Brother could hear a fly sneeze from a hundred miles away. Second Brother could spot that very fly sneezing away on the Great Wall of China. Third Brother lifted mountains that got in his way. Fourth Brother had bones of iron and Fifth Brother, legs that grew. Sixth Brother kept warm by sitting in fires, and Seventh Brother always tried to stay cheerful because when he was unhappy, it took him only a single teardrop to drown an entire village!

This tale relates how each brother was able to use his special powers to accomplish a very difficult task.

The Wizard of Oz

L. Frank Baum

Here are vocabulary words found in the story. Put a 1 in front of a word if that word is an *object*. Put a 2 in front of the word if the word is a *person*; a 3 if the word is a *plant*; and a 4 if the word is an *animal*. Guess if you do not know. Then read the paragraphs below to support or disprove guesses.

1. _____ greensward

2. _____ kalidah

3. _____ mendiant

4. _____ peplos

5. _____ snood

6. _____ counterpane

7. _____ caroche

8. _____ Winkies

9. _____ Boq

10. _____ kerrias

Outside the gates of the Emerald City, people dropped coins into the hat of the poor mendicant. Then the gates opened to admit a caroche pulled by four green horses. The landscape of lush greensward dotted with yellow, rose-like kerrias resembled a huge counterpane spread across a bed.

Boq, the Wizard's servant, greeted Dorothy. He told her of the dreaded western part of Oz, so cold that the Winkies who lived there had to wear snoods on their heads and peplos around their shoulders to keep warm. He also told of the horrible Kalidahs with bodies of bears and tiger heads. These dangers and more would await her if she ventured from the Emerald City.

COMPARE

Identify similarities and differences.

1. Select a basis for comparison.
   Examples: size, shape, uses, order,
   behavior

2. Describe the features or characteristics to
   be compared.

3. Describe similarities and differences.

4. Summarize major similarities and
   differences.

COMPARE

In *The Wizard of Oz* by L. Frank Baum, Dorothy is lifted up by a cyclone and taken to the Land of Oz, which is very different from her home in Kansas.

USE THE FIVE SENSES PATTERN TO COMPARE KANSAS TO OZ AND TO THE PLACE WHERE YOU LIVE.

If I visited the Kansas prairie

I would see_____

And I would hear_____

I would taste_____

I would smell _____

And I would feel like _____

If I visited the Land of Oz

I would see _____

And I would hear_____

I would taste_____

I would smell _____

And I would feel like_____

If I visited _____

I would see _____

And I would hear_____

I would taste_____

I would smell _____

And I would feel like _____

COMPARE

ABOUT SIMILES

A simile compares two things. "He was as tall as a tree" or "the day was as gloomy as a haunted house" are similes. Authors use similes to create mind pictures for the reader. A simile uses the words *like* or *as* in the comparison.

The Wizard of Oz by L. Frank Baum begins with a cyclone. Complete these lines using a simile to describe the cyclone that lifted Dorothy's house and carried it to Oz.

The low wail of the wind sounded
like_____

_____

_____

The grass bowed and moved in ripples
like_____

_____

_____

The cyclone had a long, dusty, gray funnel
that dipped down and touched the ground
like_____

_____

_____

The whirling winds attacked the farm

like_____

_____

_____

The house whirled around and around
like_____

_____

_____

The witch flew by Dorothy's window
like_____

_____

_____

What comparisons or similes can you think of to describe the Wicked Witch of the West?

COMPREHENSION

Comprehension requires establishing relationships among ideas. In addition, relationships are summarized or interpreted.

1. Remember, recall, or read information on a topic.

2. Relate the information to previous knowledge.

3. Explain and/or summarize the information.

4. Interpret the relationship between the information and previous knowledge.

5. Encode the information in a new form.

COMPREHENSION

Read the tale that follows. Answer the comprehension questions.

The Bell of Atri
Adapted by Nancy Polette

In the mountains of Italy there is a small village, and in the village there is a magnificent bell. Now, the villagers usually get along with each other quite well, but should a wrong be done, the person who has been wronged has merely to ring the bell. Upon hearing the bell, the villagers all gather around to listen and to decide what can be done to right the wrong. After many years the rope on the bell rotted away, and the villagers sent away for a very long rope. The new rope must be long enough for the smallest person to reach. To serve until the new rope arrived, a long vine was cut and attached to the bell.

Now, just outside the village lived a mean man. His faithful donkey who had worked hard and served him for many years was his only companion. But the donkey was old and could no longer work, so the man beat him and chased him away. When the donkey wandered into the town, what did he find but a delicious vine waiting to be eaten. As the donkey nibbled the vine, the bell began to ring. "The donkey has been wronged," the villagers cried, seeing how old and thin the poor beast was. "The wrong must be righted!" And the mean man was brought to town and ordered to put aside half of his gold for the care of the donkey, who for the rest of his days had a warm stall and plenty to eat.

1. What events led to the ringing of the bell by the donkey?
2. Name three ways that this tale is like the tale of *Hansel and Gretel*.
3. What does the story say about the mistreatment of animals?
4. What justification does the author give for taking half the man's gold?
5. Suppose the donkey had not rung the bell. What might have happened to the donkey?

COMPREHENSION OF A VISUAL

OBJECTIVE QUESTIONS

1. What shapes or sizes do you remember?
2. What characters do you remember seeing?
3. What objects, sounds, or textures do you recall?

REFLECTIVE QUESTIONS

4. Whom did you like or dislike in the picture?
5. With whom did you identify?
6. What emotions did you see in the picture?

INTERPRETATIVE QUESTIONS

7. Did any part of the picture make you feel happy? sad? apprehensive? angry? disappointed?
8. If you could change any part of the picture, what would you change?
9. If you could eliminate one thing from the picture, what would it be? Why?

DECISIONAL QUESTIONS

10. How do you think the characters in the picture feel?
11. Have you ever felt like this?
12. Who needs to see this picture? (Think of a another character from literature, TV, or film.)
13. If you could be any of the characters, which would you choose to be?

CONCEPTUALIZE

Identify common characteristics among a group of objects.

1. State the concept.

2. Give examples.

3. Give non-examples.

4. Identify defining characteristics.

5. State or write a definition of the concept.

DEVELOPING A CONCEPT

CONCEPT: FANTASY

Examples: *The Little Prince*
Charlotte's Web
Cricket in Times Square

Non-examples: *Bridge to Terabithia*
Single Shard
Where the Red Fern Grows

Characteristics: Longer than a fairy tale
Uses metaphor to
comment on society
Unreal elements
Hidden meanings
Creates belief in the unbelievable

Definition: A fantasy is a long story which reveals hidden meanings using metaphor as well as unreal characters, settings, and/or situations.

Exercise: Select one concept and develop it below: Legend, Myth, Fable, Fairy Tale

Concept: _____

Examples: _____
_____
_____

Non-examples: _____
_____
_____

Characteristics: _____
_____
_____
_____
_____

Definition: _____
_____
_____
_____

DEVELOPING A CONCEPT: FANTASY

This rap is based on the novel, *The BFG* by Roald Dahl (Farrar, 1982). What elements of fantasy can you identify in the rap? Circle the fantasy elements.

Sophie was a child snug in bed at night
Along came a giant and gave her a fright
Snatched her up though she tried to hide
And took off fast with a ten mile stride.

Look, Sophie, look, how the giant moves as fast as light
Look, Sophie, look, it's a most fantastic sight.

So Sophie made friends with the BFG
Who was always as hungry as he could be
Snozcumbers for breakfast was all he had
They tasted just awful, they really were bad.

Look, Sophie, look, all the other giants are not so sweet
Look, Sophie, look, little children they will eat!

So before the awful giants made the London scene,
   Sophie and her friend went to see the Queen
Told her of the danger that was ever so near
The Queen shook her head and said, "Never fear."

Up, Sophie, up, see the helicopters in the sky
Up, Sophie, up, see the awful giants fly.

So the army caught the giants before they could hit
And dropped them one by one in a great big pit.
Then the Queen and Sophie and the BFG
Sat down together to a lovely tea.

Smile, Sophie, smile, for the giants now have gone away.
Smile, Sophie, smile, its a "splender-if-us" day.

CREATIVE THINKING

FOUR STAGES

PREPARATION

Collecting background information for the problem under consideration.

INCUBATION

Relaxing, allowing images from the unconscious to surface.

ILLUMINATION

Comes sudddenly and unexpectedly: The "aha!" stage.

VERIFICATION

Testing, proving, or carrying out the idea to see whether it works.

CREATIVE THINKING

In *Harry Potter and the Sorcerer's Stone*, J. K. Rowling uses her creative mind to dream up these characters:

Harry Potter, a small, skinny wizard with round glasses held together with scotch tape.

Rubeus Hagrid, a giant twice as tall and five times as wide as any man.

Minerva McGonagall, a professor who can turn her desk into a pig.

Lord Voldemort, a wicked wizard who can take possession of another person's body.

Poevsi, a poltergeist who plays tricks and floats cross-legged in the air.

Sir Nicholas de Mimsy Porpington, a ghost who can flip his head off and on his neck.

EXERCISE **YOUR** CREATIVE BRAIN

1. Be a fluent thinker.
   Choose one character above and list as many appropriate names for that character as you can.

   _____   _____

   _____   _____

   _____   _____

2. Be a flexible thinker.
   How many ways can you group the names listed above? Label the groups.

   _____   _____

   _____   _____

   _____   _____

   _____   _____

3. Be an original thinker.
   Create a new character for Hogwarts School. Briefly describe the character here. Give the character an unusual name.

   _____

   _____

   _____

   _____

CREATIVE THINKING

The Wide Window by Lemony Snicket, HarperCollins, 2000.

About the book: The Baudelaire orphans — Violet, 14; Klaus, 12; and Sunny (still an infant) — go to Lake Lachrymose (right next to Damocles Dock) to live with their Aunt Josephine. She's afraid of just about everything in her house (including the telephone, the stove, the sofa, the door knobs, and realtors). Her house is built on stilts overlooking Lake Lachrymose, which is filled with man-eating leeches.

WORD GAME

To create interesting settings, the author combines words in unusual ways. What, for instance would you expect to see happen on a Fickle Ferry, a Damocles Dock, or at the Rancorous Rocks? Create a story setting by choosing one adjective and one noun. What would you expect might happen to the orphans in that setting?

Fickle	Wicked	Beach	Mansion
Rancorous	Lavender	Whirlpool	Carnival
Vile	Miserable	Garden	Sailboat
Odorous	Curdled	Lighthouse	Lane
Sneaky	Grimy	Cafe	Cave
Sinister		Rocks	

Example: The orphans might lead Count Olaf through a **Sinister Garden,** which would be overgrown with poison ivy. The orphans would be covered from head to toe to avoid contact with the plant and escape while the Count is scratching his rash.

_____

_____

_____

_____

CREATIVE THINKING

In the *Harry Potter* series by J. K. Rowling, the author creates many unusual situations, from riding on firebolts, which are high-performance broomsticks, to meeting Parslemouths, who are wizards who can talk to snakes. In order to create new characters, places and objects, the author must also create new words. You, too, can be creative by playing with words in a different way. Look at the words that follow. Choose two and combine them to make a new compound word. Then tell what this new thing will do. Create an illustrated dictionary of new words.

bridge	foot	break	wind
cast	broad	box	mail
man	porch	sun	work
home	water	rain	book
note	fish	cat	pick
tooth	light	flash	leader
cheer	time	supper	board
card	sty	pig	sauce
apple	worm	meal	

Example: Combine *foot* and *pick* to make the new word *footpick*.

When a wizard wants to dig up his gold, he says magic words to turn his foot into a pick and starts digging.

Your Word _____

Definition _____

_____

Your Word _____

Definition _____

_____

41

CRITICAL THINKING

The ability to appraise ideas, proposals, points of view, procedures, activities, behaviors, statements, positions, or issues.

1   Decide what is to be judged.

2. Use appropriate standards.

3. Gather evidence showing the extent to which the standards are met.

4. Consider evidence and make a judgment.

CRITICAL THINKING

When L. Frank Baum wrote *The Wizard of Oz*, the Tin Woodman wanted a heart, and heart transplants were still unheard of.

Scientists now predict that in the future

   A. Frozen organ banks will supply whatever organ a person needs.

   B. Replacement organs will be grown from the patient's own cells.

   C. Bionic arms and legs and artificial ears will become common.

   D. Paralyzed people will use brain waves to activate switches, thus being able to turn on TV sets or computers just by thinking.

   E. Wires from a TV camera to a blind person's brain will allow that person to see.

   F. It may be possible to reduce or eliminate aging by using antioxidants.

List four standards that should be considered in deciding the benefit to people of any new scientific discovery.

1. _____

2. _____

3. _____

4. _____

Apply the standards to each of the scientific breakthroughs listed above.

Reorder the list by placing the one that most well meets the standards first, and the one that least well meets the standards last.

_____

_____

_____

_____

_____

_____

CRITICAL THINKING

List five standards you think should be considered in hiring a new fifth grade teacher. Rank order your list from the most important item to least important item.

1. _____
2. _____
3. _____
4. _____
5. _____

Apply the standards using the information about these characters from *The Hobbit* by J.R.R. Tolkein. Rank order the characters from the one you think best meets the standards for a good teacher, to the one you think least well meets the standards. 1=best, 11=worst.

( ) **Bilbo Baggins:** An ordinary hobbit, fond of food and comfort but capable of being brave and resourceful in a crisis.

( ) **Gandalf:** a good wizard and the conductor of the entire affair. He uses his wizard's skills to fight evil forces.

( ) **Thorin Oakenshield:** The leader of the dwarves and heir to the title "King Under the Mountain." He is overcome by greed but sees the error of his ways before dying.

( ) **Elrond:** Elrond is an old elf and a gracious host who lives in Rivendell.

( ) **Beorn:** The skin-changing man who lives near the edge of Mirkwood. He gives the travelers shelter and supplies when they show up at his home.

( ) **Bombur:** Bombur is the fat dwarf who often messes things up.

( ) **Bard:** Bard is a descendant of the royal line of Dale who makes a brave stand against Smaug with a small group of townspeople, and leads an army of men to Lonely Mountain with the Elvenking.

( ) **Dain:** He becomes king after Thorin dies, and is a very fine leader.

( ) **Lord of the Eagles:** The leader of the eagles who helps the travelers escape from the Wargs.

( ) **Bolg:** The son of the Great Goblin, who seeks revenge against Bilbo and party.

( ) **Smaug:** The dragon of Lonely Mountain, an arrogant and hateful beast who loves treasure only for the sake of having it.

DECISION-MAKING

Deciding among objects or alternatives.

1. List objects or alternatives to choose from.

2. Establish critria for selection.

3. Check each alternative or object to see if it meets the criteria.

4. Select the action(s) or description(s) that best meets the criteria.

DECISION-MAKING

The Three Robbers by Tomi Ungerer, Atheneum, 1962.

BOOKTALK

The three robbers choked and sputtered when Tiffany asked them what all of their treasures were for. They decided to use their fortune to help abandoned children.

Suppose that you have just inherited $5,000.00. You are faced with the same problem as the robbers. You must make a decision. What will you do with all of your money? You will use some for yourself, but how could you also use it to help others?

List different plans for your money under ALTERNATIVES. Then list the standards you want your decision to meet under CRITERIA. Score your alternatives with the scale provided.

SPEND IT WISELY				
SCALE 5 = excellent choice 3 = average choice 1 = poor choice	**CRITERIA**			
ALTERNATIVES				
	Help more than one person?			
Buy a lifetime supply of candy				

Your many friends will be more than happy to help you carry out your decision to spend your money. Just list your decision on the back of this paper and explain to them why you chose it.

DECISION-MAKING

The Bunyip of Berkeley's Creek by Jenny Wagner, Bradbury, 1973.

How To Beautify a Bunyip!

The Bunyip of Berkeley's Creek has just waddled into The Bright-n-Beautiful Beauty/Barber Shop. As the owner and operator, you are faced with quite a decision! What will you do to improve the poor Bunyip's appearance?

Being so creatively talented in this area of work, you should be able to list many different solutions to this problem. These solutions could range from a haircut to a facelift! Please list your ideas under ALTERNATIVES. The CRITERIA that you want your solutions to meet have been conveniently provided for you, along with a scale on which to weigh the solutions.

B-n-B's					
Scale	**CRITERIA**				
5 = excellent choice 4 = above avg choice 3 = average choice 2 = below avg choice 1 = poor choice	Fast?	Easy?	Cheap?	Effective?	Total score
ALTERNATIVES					
Dye its fur green	2	2	3	3	10

What is your best solution? And why?_____

_____

_____

DEDUCTIVE THINKING

From Generalization to Supporting Data

1. Examine the generalization.

2. Seek supporting data, cases, or evidence.

3. Seek sources of additional supporting data.

4. Find supporting data in the sources.

5. Apply to the generalization.

DEDUCTIVE THINKING

What evidence can you find in the booktalk below for the following statements?

1. At the end of the book, the boy's world is one of carpets and table legs.

---

2. At the beginning of the story, the boy has no choice but to go to Norway.

---

3. Grandmama is a very smart woman.

---

4. The hotel people do not recognize the women as witches.

---

5. After consuming Formula 86, one must remain a mouse for life.

BOOKTALK

The Witches by Roald Dahl, Johnathan Cape Publishers, London, 1983.

A young boy loses both of his parents in an automobile accident. He is sent to live with his grandmother in Norway. She tells him about witches and the powers that they possess and instructs him in ways to identify a witch. The boy and his Grandmama return to England in order for the boy to complete his education. While working on his new treehouse he has an encounter with a real witch. Grandmama suddenly becomes ill with pneumonia. The doctors advise a summer holiday in Bournemouth at the Hotel Magnificent. While wandering around the hotel, the boy gets trapped in a meeting of witches in disguise and overhears the plan of the Grand High Witch to rid the world of children by turning them into mice. The witches try their Formula 86 Delayed Action Mouse Maker on Bruno Jenkins, a boy who is also a guest at the Hotel Magnificent. Bruno turns into a mouse after eating a chocolate bar laced with the Formula 86!

Just when the boy thinks he's in the clear, the witches catch him. They zap him into a mouse just like Bruno Jenkins. Now that he is a mouse, the boy believes that life will be a lot more interesting. Grandmama lowers the boy out the terrace door in a half-knitted sock to the Grand High Witch's window. The boy is to get into the room and steal a bottle of Formula 86. The Grand High Witch comes in at the wrong moment and the boy barely escapes. The boy and his Grandmama try to devise a plan to beat the witches at their own game. They decide to use the Formula 86 to turn the witches into mice but are not quite sure how they will manage to do this.

The boy sneaks into the kitchen and sprinkles the Formula 86 in the pot of soup made especially for the witches. The witches do eat the soup and are instantly transformed into mice. The boy (who is still a mouse) and his grandmother return to Norway. Grandmama invents gadgets to make the boy's life easier.

DEDUCTIVE THINKING

Here are deductive thinking questions that can be applied to any fairy tale or fantasy.

1. **Memory: recalling information**
Who did _____?
When did _____?
How many_____?
What are _____?

2. **Definitions**
What is meant by _____?
What meaning did you understand
for _____?
Define _____.

3. **Generalizations: finding common characteristics in a group of ideas or things.**
What events led to _____?
Name thee ways that _____ resembles _____.
What caused _____ to _____?

Example: Fairy Tale: *Snow White and the Seven Dwarves*

1. Who took Snow White into the forest?

   When did the wicked queen discover that Snow White was alive?

   How many dwarves were there?

   What are the characters' names?

2. What is meant by by treachery?

3. What events led to Snow White eating the apple?

   Name three ways that the story of Snow White is like the story of Cinderella.

   What caused the wicked queen to dislike Snow White?

ELABORATION

Adding details to an existing concept.

1. Carefully examine the concept to be elaborated.

2. What is the main idea?

3. Decide if you want to add details to embellish the idea or to change the idea.

4. Add appropriate details.

ELABORATION

Harry Potter and the Sorcerer's Stone by J. K. Rowling
Illustrations by Mary Grandpré
Arthur A. Levine Books, Scholastic Press, 1997

Harry Potter has never been the star of a Quidditch team, in which one scores points while riding a broom far above the ground. He knows no spells, has never helped to hatch a dragon, and has never worn a cloak of invisibility.

All he knows is a miserable life with the Dursleys, his horrible aunt and uncle, and their abominable son, Dudley, a great, big, swollen, spoiled bully. Harry's room is in a tiny closet at the foot of the stairs, and he hasn't had a birthday party in eleven years.

But all that is about to change when a mysterious letter arrives by owl messenger. The letter is an invitation to an incredible place that Harry will find unforgettable. For it is at Hogwarts School of Witchcraft and Wizardry that Harry finds not only friends, aerial sports, and magic in everything from classes to meals, but a great destiny that's been waiting for him if he can survive the encounter.

Suppose the owl got tired of delivering mail. He wants to take up another profession. Elaborate on this picture to show the owl in his new role.

Ideas: What if the owl were a rock star? a football player? an opera singer?

Variation: What would the owl look like if he were "Owl Wet" or "Owl Mixed Up"?

ELABORATION

These people have just seen the movie *Harry Potter and the Sorcerer's Stone.* Elaborate on the picture by adding comments and facial expressions to show each person's reaction to the movie.

ELABORATION

What could you add to little pig's straw house so that the wolf would not be able to blow it down?

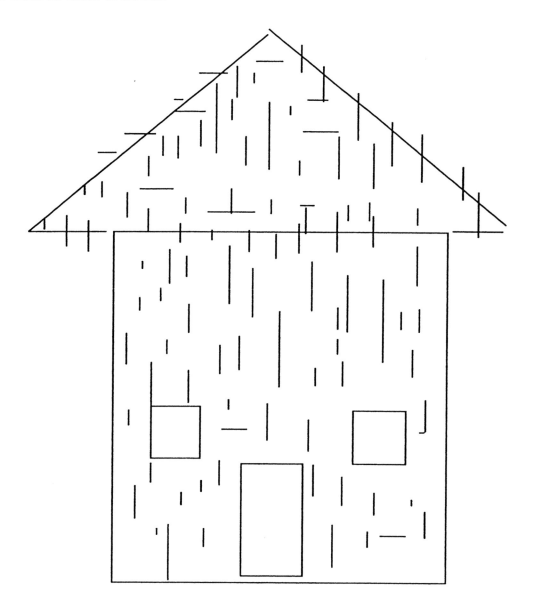

EVALUATION

To make a judgment of the merit or worth of an activity, object, or idea.

1. Identify what is to be evaluated.

2. Define standards of appraisal.

3. Collect data related to each standard.

4. Collect an equal number of positive and negative points to avoid prejudice.

5. Make a judgment.

EVALUATE

You are wandering in the woods alone. It is a warm day and you stop beside a cool spring to take a drink. Just as your lips are about to touch the water you are stopped from drinking by a young boy. He explains that the spring contains the power of youth. Those who drink from it will have life everlasting. He suggests that you wait a few years and then drink the water. When you reach the age of seventeen, life everlasting will seem like a great idea. Or will it?

See: *Tuck Everlasting* by Natalie Babbitt, Farrar, Straus & Giroux, New York, 1975.

EVALUATE: Should those who discover the spring drink from it?

REASONS TO DRINK	REASONS NOT TO DRINK
_____	_____
_____	_____
_____	_____
_____	_____
_____	_____
_____	_____
_____	_____
_____	_____
_____	_____

Something to think about: If you had one bottle of the Magic Water and decided not to drink it, what would you do with it?

EVALUATE

The year is 1883. You are a member of Professor Sherman's balloon crew. On the seventh day of your voyage over the ocean, a seagull dives into your balloon and you are forced to land on the Island of Krakatoa. The twenty families who live on the island want to keep secret their ownership of the most valuable diamond mine in the world. They are determined to keep you and the other crew members on the island forever. You are supplied with every comfort and treated with kindness and courtesy, but you are carefully guarded to prevent your escape.

Should you or should you not attempt to escape?

REASONS TO ESCAPE	REASONS TO STAY
_____	_____
_____	_____
_____	_____
_____	_____
_____	_____
_____	_____
_____	_____
_____	_____

Examine both lists. Your decision will be _____

_____

Read: *The Twenty-One Balloons* by William Pené duBois, New York, Viking, 1947.

FLUENCY/FLEXIBILITY

Finding new categories or uses, stretching the mind beyond the usual or expected response.

1. Define the area to be examined.

2. Examine using all five senses. How would it feel, smell, taste, look, or sound?

3. Use questions that begin with:

   How many ways _____?
   What if _____?
   Suppose that _____?
   What if you were _____ ?
   How is _____ like _____ ?

4. Observe carefully. How many different ways do people do things? Say things? Make use of things?

FLUENCY

SURROUND THE LETTER M WITH WORDS THAT BEGIN WITH M AND ARE RELATED TO THE LETTER IN SOME WAY.

FLUENCY/FLEXIBILITY

Just Suppose!

In *Harold's Fairy Tale* by Crockett Johnson (HarperCollins, 1956), Harold discovers that a giant witch is stopping the flowers from growing in an enchanted garden. To drive the witch from the garden, Harold uses mosquitos, smoke, fire, and rain.

Just suppose: The Giant Witch

1. Killed all the mosquitos with a giant fly swatter?

2. Blew out the fire?

3. Drank all the rain?

What other ideas can you give Harold for getting rid of the witch? Remember, they have to be things he can really do.

List your ideas here. Circle the one you think is the best idea.

IDEAS

1. _____

2. _____

3. _____

4. _____

5. _____

FLUENCY/FLEXIBILITY

The Great Big Enormous Turnip by Alexi Tolstoy

In this tale, a man has a turnip in his garden that is so large he cannot pull it up alone. His wife, his children, and all the neighbors have to help before the turnip finally comes out of the ground.

Think of how expensive it must have been for the old man to pull that great big enormous turnip! He probably had to pay all of those helpers. Since he obviously has a green thumb, he will more than likely grow another turnip as big as the first one.

As an expert gardener, and a member of the "Great Growers' Green Garden Group," you should be able to help the old man!

Put on your fluent thinking cap. List ten or more possible solutions for getting the huge turnip out of the old man's garden.

1. _____
2. _____
3. _____
4. _____
5. _____
6. _____
7. _____
8. _____
9. _____
10. _____

Which of the above solutions would be the easiest and why?

_____

_____

FORECASTING

Determining action based on
cause and effect.

1. Consider all possible causes of a given situation.

2. Consider all possible effects of a given situation.

3. Choose the best cause and effect.

4. Determine the appropriate action(s) based on the choice.

5. Give reasons for choosing the action.

FORECASTING

Looking at Cause and Effect

A WOLF IN SHEEP'S CLOTHING
AN AESOP'S FABLE

One spring day a wolf bounded up over a hill and came upon a flock of sheep. The wolf was very very hungry, so he rolled and rolled on the ground among the flock until he was covered with the white fluffy wool that had dropped from the backs of the sheep. Now that he looked like a sheep, he could kill and eat one whenever he pleased. The wolf grew fat and lazy, for he did not have to work for his dinner.

One evening the shepherd, who was very hungry, decided to kill one of the sheep for food. Since the wolf in sheep's clothing was so fat, he could not run as fast as the others. Thus the shepherd caught him first, killed him, and cooked him up for dinner.

Complete these sentences: (Give at least two effects for each cause.)

Because the hungry wolf saw some sheep, (1) _____

_____

(2)_____

_____

Because the wolf was covered with white, fluffy wool, (1)_____

_____

(2) _____

_____

Because the wolf grew fat and lazy, (1) _____

_____

(2)_____

_____

Because the shepherd was hungry, (1) _____

_____

(2) _____

_____

FORECASTING

The Sleeping Bread
by Stefan Czernecki and Timothy Rhodes, Hyperion, 1992.

BOOKTALK

This is the tale of the village of San Pedro and of two men who were important to the life of the town. Beto was a cheerful baker who mixed bread dough every night and baked and sold the golden loaves by day. Zafiro was a ragged beggar who knew that when he was hungry, kind Beto would have crusts of bread to share.

A festival was to be celebrated, with many visitors coming to San Pedro. Therefore the townsfolk decided that all beggars should be banished from the village.

As Zafiro bade Beto a tearful goodbye, a tear fell into the water jar used in mixing the bread dough. The next morning Beto was shocked to see the bread would not rise. Not even prodding or praying would help. Has the village lost more than just a beggar? Or is there a way to awaken the sleeping bread?

List possible causes preventing the baker's bread from rising.

_____

_____

_____

List the effects of the villagers having no bread for the festival.

_____

_____

_____

_____

What is the most likely cause?

_____

_____

How can the villagers get bread again?

_____

_____

GENERALIZING

To make a statement based on evidence that applies to a group.

1. Collect, organize, and examine the data about the group.

2. Identify the common characteristics of the group members.

3. Make and state a generalization that applies to the group, based on the common characteristics.

4. Find other instances in which the generalization is true.

5. Try to transfer the generalization to other situations or uses.

GENERALIZING

Here are some generalizations about fairy tales and fantasy. Before each statement, write YES if the generalization is true. Write NO if it is not true. For each NO answer, write the title of one fairy tale or fantasy and one fact about that story that disproves the generalization.

Example:

1. __NO__ Giants are always bad characters who want to do harm to people.

The giant in *The BFG* by Roald Dahl is a good giant who helps a little girl.

2. _____ Fairy tale princesses are always sweet and kind.

_____

3. _____ Wolves are sneaky creatures who want to eat something or someone.

_____

4. _____ The only numbers found in fairy tale titles are three and seven.

_____

5. _____ The only fruit found in a fairy tale is an apple.

_____

6. _____ The only flower found in a fairy tale is a rose.

_____

7. _____ The youngest son usually wins the prize or the hand of the princess.

_____

8. _____ All fairy tales begin with "Once upon a time."

_____

GENERALIZING

Support or disprove the following generalization.

Good characters in fairy tales are attractive to look at.

Bad or evil characters in fairy tales are ugly.

Find four fairy tales. Complete the boxes below.

Title/Character	Four words that describe the good character	Four words that describe the bad character

After comparing the data from the four tales, what general statement can you make about the relationship of character and appearance?

_____
_____
_____
_____

GROUPING

To bring together items with
similar characteristics.

1. Observe and gather information about the
   items to be grouped.

2. Look for similar qualities or characteristics.

3. Find ways that some of the items are alike.

4. Sort similar items into groups and label
   each group.

GROUPS AND SUBGROUPS

List as many animals as you can that are found on or around a farm.

hen   horse
duck   cow

_____	_____
_____	_____
_____	_____
_____	_____
_____	_____
_____	_____
_____	_____
_____	_____
_____	_____

Group the animals in several ways. Follow the pattern to show the comparisons.

Group label: FUNCTION

A cow provides food.
A hen provides food.
A duck provides food.
A horse does not provide food.

Group label: _____
A _____ can _____
A _____ can _____
A _____ can _____
A _____ cannot _____

Group Label: _____
A _____ can _____
A _____ can _____
A _____ can _____
A _____ cannot _____

Group label: _____
A _____ has _____
A _____ has _____
A _____ has _____
A _____does not have
_____

Group Label: _____
A _____ has _____
A _____ has _____
A _____ has _____
A _____does not have _____

Group label: _____
A _____ has _____
A _____ has _____
A _____ has_____
A _____ does not have
_____

GROUPING

Swamp Angel by Anne Isaacs.
Illustrated by Paul O. Zelinsky. Dutton, 1994.

When Angelica Longrider was born, she was scarcely taller than her mother and couldn't climb a tree without help. She was a full two years old before she built her first log cabin. But by the time she was fully grown, Swamp Angel, as she was known, could lasso a tornado and drink an entire lake dry. She single-handedly saved the settlers from the fearsome bear known as Thundering Tarnation, wrestling him from the top of the Great Smoky Mountains to the bottom of a deep lake. It was a fight that lasted five days. When both Swamp Angel and the bear were too tired to fight, they went to sleep and Swamp Angel's snores were so loud that she snored down a huge tree, which landed on the bear and killed it. Swamp Angel paid tribute to her foe and then had enough bear meat to feed everyone in Tennessee.

Put these words from *Swamp Angel* into groups. Label each group.

woodswoman	Tennessee	buckskin	swamp
settlers	homespun	pioneers	wilderness
appetite	gobble	thundering	tarnation
wily	desperate	competition	reward
enormous	reputation	dewdrops	taunt
trail	molasses	approach	hickory
varmint	commenced	obliged	nightfall
determined	tornado	twister	lasso
bristled	wrestled	mountains	gigantic
tobacco	snored	locomotive	thunderstorm
rockslide	blunders	slurped	praise

HYPOTHESIZE

To state a tentative explanation, solution, or proposition that defines a relationship between two or more processes or items.

1. State a preliminary hypothesis that explains observed relationships.

2. State reasons for the hypothesis.

3. Refine the statement so that it can be tested.

4. Identify essential conditions and procedures for testing.

5. Analyze test results to see if the hypothesis is supported by evidence.

HYPOTHESIZE

A hypothesis is a statement that may or may not be true. Testing the hypothesis will determine whether or not it is true.

EXAMPLE: Hypothesis: The favorite kind of book of students in my class is fantasy.

Reasons: A lot of students in my class check out fantasy titles from the library. Everyone enjoys it when the teacher reads aloud from a fantasy.

To Test: Conduct a poll. Ask each student for his/her favorite kind of book.

Student	fantasy	real life stories	mysteries	animal stories	historical fiction	science fiction

Conclusion: The favorite kind of book of students in my class is _____

IMAGINATION

An essential tool of the human intellect.

WITH IT WE CAN

  INVENT NEW REALITIES

  FORM MENTAL IMAGES

  MAKE UP CHARACTERS

  LOOK INTO THE FUTURE

  BRING THE PAST BACK TO LIFE

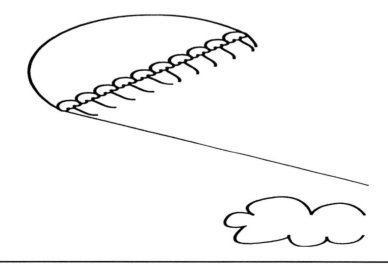

73

USE YOUR IMAGINATION

Answer the questions about this picture

What is the bear's name?_____

Where the bear sleeping? _____

What caused the bear to go to sleep?_____

_____

How long has the bear been asleep?_____

_____

Are there any other bears, animals, or people nearby? _____

_____

What will awaken the bear? _____

What will the bear do when it wakes up? _____

_____

IMAGINATION

USE YOUR IMAGINATION TO CREATE A SPACE-AGE CINDERELLA.

1. What would her name be? _____

2. Name her sisters. _____ and _____

3. Where would they live? _____

4. What jobs would she have to do? _____

_____

5. Who would the sisters want to marry? _____

6. What would be the big event everyone wants to attend?

_____

7. Who will help her? _____

8. What will she lose? _____

Begin your story here. Continue on the back of the page.

Once upon a time there was a poor girl named _____

_____. She lived in a _____

with her mean stepsisters _____and _____.

She worked from dawn to dusk doing _____

and _____ and _____

The mean stepsisters received an invitation to _____

given by _____. Off they went wearing their finest

_____. Poor _____ was left in

the _____ to cook _____

for a big feast on the next day. Then _____ arrived in a

_____.

"Do not be sad," she said. "You will go to the _____."

75

INDUCTIVE REASONING

From Data to Generalization

1. Collect, organize, and examine data.

2. Identify common elements or what is generally true.

3. State a generalization based on common or similar elements.

4. Check against additional data to see whether the generalization holds up.

INDUCTIVE REASONING

Tikki Tikki Tembo, retold by Arlene Mosel
Illustrated by Blair Lent
Henry Holt & Co., New York, 1968

Long ago the Chinese gave their firstborn sons very long names. *Tikki tikki tembo-nosa rembo-chari bari ruchi-pip peri pembo* is the full name of a boy who falls in a well. When his younger brother attempts to get help, he has a hard time saying the long name, and help is delayed with surprising results.

CATCH THE CLUE

Use the following clues to discover the mystery word. Students will select a number from one to ten. Read the clue for that number, and allow the student to guess or pass. The game continues until the mystery word is guessed or all clues have been read.

1. You can do it alone.

2. You usually handle more than one item when you do it.

3. You can do it just for yourself.

4. You can do it for others.

5. You must use flour to do it.

6. An oven is needed to do it.

7. When you do it, the kitchen is filled with a good smell.

8. Bambolona's father did it.

9. You can do it every day.

10. Some people do it once a week.

Answer: baking

INDUCTIVE REASONING

PUTTING A TALE BACK TOGETHER.

These bits of history, if put in the correct order, will tell you the sad tale of a young queen.

Birth Announcement: Mr. & Mrs. Ay are proud new grandparents of a baby girl named Ankhesenamum (Ank for short).
Uncle Ay's Journal Entry: Tut will never guess the enormous power I now have!
News Headline: Nine-year-old King Tut assumes throne. Uncle to act as advisor.
News Headline: Mysterious Death of 18-year old Tut.
Marriage Announcement: 17-year-old Tut marries Ank and makes her his queen.
Conversation between Tut and Wife: "It is time I began to rule the land. Uncle Ay must go."
Death Notice: Mrs. Ay dies.
Marriage Announcement: Ay, advisor to deceased King Tut, marries King's widow and becomes the new king.

Who did Ank marry first?

Was King Tut murdered? If so, by whom?

Who was Ank's second husband?

INFERRING

Drawing a possible consequence, conclusion, or implication from a set of facts and premises.

Questions for inferential thinking:

1. Why do you suppose that _____?

2. What do you suppose someone should do?

3. What do you think was meant by _____? Why?

4. What evidence can you cite for the inference?

INFERRING

THE ALLEGORY: INFERRING MEANING BEYOND THE OBVIOUS

King Midas, cured of his love of riches, now seeks the simple life. He spends his time with the shepherds and nymphs, and sometimes with the gods who come to earth for rustic pleasures. On one occasion, Midas is selected to judge a music contest between the god Apollo, playing on his golden lyre, and the god Pan, playing on his reed pipe.

Having no ear for music, Midas tactlessly awards the prize to Pan. Angrily, Apollo exclaims, "Midas, you deserve the ears of a donkey!" Instantly, Midas's ears grow long and pointed and ridiculous.

Midas is terribly ashamed of his foolish appearance and wears a turban to hide his affliction. However, when his hair grows uncomfortably long, Midas summons a barber and swears him to secrecy. The barber promises to keep Midas's secret.

Finally, unable to remain silent any longer, the barber goes to a nearby field, digs a hole, and into it whispers, "King Midas has donkey's ears." Then he covers up the hole and goes away.

The following spring, a clump of reeds grows from the hole. With every breeze the reeds whisper, "King Midas has donkey's ears."

WHAT EVIDENCE CAN YOU CITE TO SUPPORT THESE INFERENCES:

1. King Midas was a vain person. _____

_____

2. Those who chose the music judges applied no standards for their choices.

_____

3. Apollo was unjust for punishing King Midas.

_____

4. Keeping a secret is difficult.

_____

5. King Midas will refuse to judge any future music contests.

_____

INFERRING

The Iron Giant: A Story In Five Nights,

by Ted Hughes, Faber & Faber, Ltd., 1985.

BOOKTALK

A huge iron man appears from nowhere. He is so intent on listening and looking that he steps off a high cliff, scattering his body parts on the beach below. With the help of seagulls he puts himself back together and sets off looking for something to eat. Hogarth, a farmer's son, sees the giant and tells his father. Many of the other farmers don't believe in the giant until their farm machinery disappears and huge footprints are found. They dig a large pit and Hogarth lures the giant into the pit where the farmers cover him with earth.

In the spring the Iron Giant pushes up out of the pit. Hogarth leads him to a junkyard where he will have plenty of metal to eat.

Meanwhile astronomers gaze at a star that turns into a terrible creature. It rushes toward Earth and lands, covering all of Australia. The creature demands food and will eat any living thing. The people of the Earth had built many terrible weapons, but none can destroy the creature. Hogarth asks the Iron Giant to help. The Iron Giant challenges the space creature to a test of strength. The Iron Giant wins the contest and the space creature is sent to live inside the moon and sing a beautiful melody that will bring peace on Earth.

INFERENTIAL QUESTIONS

1. What economic impact will the Iron Giant have on the farms if he is not stopped?

2. Why did Hogarth help the Giant when he arose from the pit in the spring?

3. What do you think the author is saying with this statement: "The people of the Earth had built many terrible weapons, but none can destroy the creature"?

4. What is the author's opinion of war?

INTERPRET

Getting meaning from a source.

1. What are the main ideas?

2. What are the supporting details?

3. What relationship do you find between

_____ and _____?

4. Explain the main idea in your own words.

INTERPRET

Fantastic Mr. Fox

by Roald Dahl, Knopf, 1970.

Fantastic Mr. Fox tells of the adventures of Mr. Fox and three farmers, Boggis, Bunce, and Bean. The farmers are rich, greedy, and disgusting villains who want to destroy the fox family. Mr. Fox, on the other hand, is a charming, clever fellow whose only crime is trying to feed his engaging family. Mr. Fox's ingenuity saves all the digging animals from starvation when they are trapped underground by the mean farmers. In the farmers' attempt to exterminate the fox family, they destroy the countryside.

The main idea of this story is _____

_____

Two details that support the main idea are

_____

_____

Tell how this story is related to one of these newspaper headlines:

SOCIAL WELFARE FUND TOPS GOAL

LARGE CROWD AT EARTH DAY CELEBRATION

PRISON OVERCROWDING A PROBLEM

LOCAL FACTORY CLOSES

MANY OPPOSE ALASKAN OIL DRILLING

INTERPRET

Show your understanding of a familiar fairy tale by creating a poem or rap.

EXAMPLE

Ashpet: An Appalachian Tale retold by Joanne Compton, Holiday House, 1994.

Ashpet is kind and Ashpet is good,
Does all the jobs that a serving girl should.
The Widow was cruel, the Widow was mean.
Told Ashpet to chop and to scrub and to clean.

(Chorus)
Work, Ashpet, work!
Get the cabin shining clean and bright.
Work, Ashpet, work!
From early morning until night.

Then came a meeting at the little mountain church
The Widow and her daughters left Ashpet in the lurch.
The girl cried tears, she felt so sad and sick
Then Granny showed up with her walking stick.

(Repeat chorus)

Granny gave the girl a dress and some shoes
Sent her off to the church, a husband to choose.
Ashpet fell in love with the doctor's son
Who found her shoe and her love he won.

Smile, Ashpet, smile!
For the Widow Hopper's gone away.
Smile, Ashpet, smile!
With the doctor's son you'll stay.

JARGON

CHARACTERISTIC IDIOMS OF A
SPECIAL ACTIVITY OR GROUP.

THE DANGER

OF JARGON

IS THAT IT CAN

BECOME A SUBSTITUTE

FOR

THINKING.

JARGON

Each profession has its own jargon.

Patients "expire."

Passengers "board" planes.

Lawyers "mediate."

Teachers are "cognitive strategists."

Here is some jargon that could be used if your profession were FAIRY TALE READER.

BONEFOOLED—Any act of fooling a witch with a chicken bone (as in *Hansel and Gretel*).

FRUIT-FLOGGED—The result of eating a poisoned apple (as in *Snow White*).

FOOL-FINGERED—The act of turning anything you touch into gold (as in *King Midas and the Golden Touch*).

HARIFIED—The act of being caught letting down unreal hair when trying to fool a witch (as in *Rapunzel*).

LISP-SHOD—The act of trying to stuff a fat foot into a tiny glass slipper (Cinderella's sisters).

Your word:

_____

Definition: _____

_____

_____

JUDGE

To make an informed evaluation based on standards.

1. Decide what is to be judged.

2. List standards that apply.

3. Gather evidence to the extent to which each standard is met.

4. Consider evidence and make a judgement.

JUDGE

A Horse With Golden Wings

You are President of the Twisting Travels Transportation Corporation. You have just heard about a new means of transportation, a horse with golden wings! What an exciting new adventure in the transportation business! If your company is the first to make flying horses available, you will make millions!

There could be some advantages and disadvantages. It could be extremely expensive to breed flying horses and provide golden wings. Therefore, it is up to you to **judge** the idea of the horse with golden wings as a new means of transportation. List as many advantages and disadvantages as possible below.

STANDARDS

1. What do people want in good transportation? Will the horse provide this?

    Mark each factor with one of the following: All of the time, Part of the time, Never

    Speed _____

    Reliability _____

    On-time schedules _____

    Safety _____

    Unique new experience _____

    Reasonable cost _____

2. List factors that you as the business owner must consider. Mark each cost *high* or *low*.

    Cost of maintaining a stable of flying horses _____

    Insurance costs _____

    Cost of a flying-horse terminal and employees _____

Now you have applied standards **as** to why or why not you will put this new product on the market. What decision will you make?

JUDGE

In *The Reptile Room* by Lemony Snicket, everyone comes running to find Sunny screaming that she has been bitten. A snake is wrapped around her. When they find the snake is not poisonous, Stephano claims that he is an expert on snakes. He is caught in a lie and the orphans hope that now Mr. Poe will know who he really is, the wicked Count Olaf.

Activity: Circle a choice. State your standard for the choice.

Would you rather ... (Circle one item in each group)

1. Have a snake for a pet? Have a skunk for a pet? Have a rat for a pet?

   Standard_____

   _____

2 Sleep three in a bed? Sleep on the floor? Sleep in a barn?

   Standard_____

   _____

3. Eat cold oatmeal? Eat hard biscuits? Do without breakfast?

   Standard_____

   _____

4. Meet Count Olaf? Meet King Kong? Meet the Wicked Witch of the West?

   Standard_____

   _____

5. Be animated? Be intimidated? Be laminated?

   Standard_____

   _____

KNOWLEDGE

In knowledge acquisition, the learner

1. Is attentive

2. Absorbs information

3. Remembers

4. Practices, drills, recites

5. Discovers information

6. Recognizes information that has already been covered

KNOWLEDGE

Demonstrate your knowledge of types of sentences and parts of speech by finding each of these types of sentences in a fairy tale of your choice.

Title of the fairy tale: _____

1. A declarative sentence:

   _____

2. An interrogative sentence:

   _____

3. A sentence that contains three or more nouns:

   _____

4. A sentence with a possessive proper noun and a singular common noun:

   _____

5. An imperative sentence:

   _____

6. A sentence with an adverb that tells how:

   _____

7. A sentence with two prepositional phrases:

   _____

8. A sentence with three nouns and two adjectives:

   _____

9. A sentence with an appositive:

   _____

10. An exclamatory sentence:

   _____

May be copied for classroom use. *Teaching Skills with Fairy Tales and Fantasy*, by Nancy Polette (Westport, CT: Teacher Ideas Press, an imprint of Libraries Unlimited). © 2005.

KNOWLEDGE

Redwall by Brian Jacques, Philomel, 1986.

BOOKTALK

It is the Summer of the Late Rose. But a sinister shadow has fallen across the ancient stone abbey of Redwall, even as the gentle mice of Mossflower Wood gather there to celebrate a year of peace and abundance. For it is rumored that Cluny is coming — Cluny, the terrible one-eyed rat, as mean as a rattlesnake, with his battle-seasoned horde — Cluny, whose vow is to conquer the renowned Redwall Abbey!

The worried woodland creatures rush to a desperate defense. But what can an abbey of peace-loving mice do against Cluny the Scourge and his army of rats? If only they had the sword of Martin the Warrior, they might have a chance of saving their beloved Abbey. But the hiding place of the legendary sword has been long forgotten, even by the wise old mouse Methuselah. It is his bumbling young apprentice Matthias who sets out to find the sword and who becomes a most unlikely hero.

Read the booktalk. Answer the knowledge questions. Write a question related to the story which is NOT a knowledge question.

1. Name the characters in the story.

   _____

2. Where did the story take place?

   _____

3. Recall the major events.

   _____

   _____

   _____

4. Find one example of literary style in the story (metaphor, alliteration, personification, simile).

   _____

5. Your question:

   _____

LOGICAL THINKING

Believed to be a left-brain function that organizes and associates ideas.

1. Begin with assumptions or first concepts.

2. Generate new ideas step-by-step.

3. Arrive at an end point or solution.

4. Each step is based on previously acquired knowledge and patterns of correct reasoning.

LOGICAL THINKING: LOGIC PUZZLE

Three sisters each had three eyes. They each had two eyes like other people and one additional eye. One had her extra eye on a finger, one had hers on a toe, and one had hers on the top of her head. Their names were Sara, Tara, and Mim.

They each also had an unusual pet dog. One dog had two tails. One had six legs, and one had wings.

One girl ate only fruit, one ate only vegetables, and one ate only meat.

Use the clues below to deduce the girls' and their dogs' special features and to find the answers to the following questions.

Who had an extra eye on her finger?

Whose dog had six legs?

Who ate only meat?

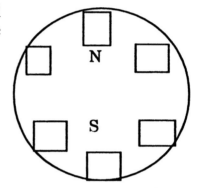

CLUES:

Sara found her extra eye was valuable when she was reaching into a tree to get her food.

Tara could see her dog above her without tipping her head.

Carrots were Min's favorite food.

The place where each girl had an extra eye is never started with the same letter as the extra body part of her dog.

	Head	Finger	Toe	Tails	Wings	Legs	Fruit	Veg.	Meat
SARA									
TARA									
MIM									

Key: Sara: finger, tails, fruit. Tara: head, wings, meat. Mim: toe, legs, vegetables.

LOGICAL THINKING: LOGIC PUZZLE

Six swans nested in a circle around a small pond. Each was either slightly larger or smaller than the others. Each guarded something she had found in the pond: a gold ring, a turquoise bead, a water lily, a silver bracelet, a glass bead, or a piece of red ribbon.

Use the clues below to find out where the swans (A, B, C, D, E, and F) nested, their relative sizes, and their treasures. Then answer the questions that follow.

CLUES: All of the swans faced the center of the pond.

Swan B nested at the south end of the pond.
Neither Swan D nor Swan F was next to her.
Her treasure was glass.
Swan A was smaller than Swan C and larger than Swan E.
She nested between Swans D and F.
Swan C had a metal treasure.
She lived to the left of Swan B and to the right of Swan F.
Swan D was larger than Swan A but smaller than Swan B.
She had the gold ring.
Swan F was larger than Swan B but smaller than Swan C.
She found a bead.
Swan A wove her ribbon into her nest.

1. Who nested at Swan D's left?
2. Who found the water lily?
3. Who was the largest swan?

	GR	TB	WL	SB	GB	RR		1	2	3	4	5	6
A													
B													
C													
D													
E													
F													

Key: 1. E, 2. E, 3. C

METAPHORICAL THINKING

Seeing a similarity in process, property, or principle between two dissimilar things.

1. Name a person, object, animal, event, or concept.

2. Ask:

   What does it look like?
   How does it function?
   What are its parts?
   How did it come to be?
   What is its process or action?
   What is its importance?
   Is it a part of something larger?

3. Ask:
   What other things have similar properties?

4. List the similarities.

5. Complete the sentence:
   _____ is a _____ because _____.

METAPHOR

In *The Wide Window* by Lemony Snicket, the children, who are trying to rescue Aunt Josephine, are caught in a hurricane.

Use metaphor to write a literary description of a hurricane.

1. Begin by choosing one of the following: the wind, the waves, the lighthouse, the sailboat.
   Example: The sailboat

2. Tell what it reminds you of (metaphor).
   The sailboat is a rocking horse.

3. Tell what it does that a person or animal does (personification).
   The sailboat is a rocking horse galloping.

4. Tell how it does it.
   The sailboat is a rocking horse galloping rapidly.

5. Tell where it does it.

   The sailboat is a rocking horse galloping rapidly over the waves.

Create your descriptive sentences about the wind, the waves, and the lighthouse.

_____

_____

_____

_____

_____

_____

_____

_____

_____

_____

_____

_____

USING METAPHOR TO DESCRIBE

On their journey to the South in *The Wizard of Oz*, Dorothy and her friends come upon a thick wood. One of the trees picks Scarecrow up in its branches and flings him headlong among his fellow travelers. When a branch bends down to grab the Tin Woodman, he cuts it in two with his ax. With the Tin Woodman chopping off the attacking branches, the group makes it safely through the forest.

A metaphor is a word or phrase that suggests a likeness between two objects.

"The branches were grasping fingers reaching for their prey."

Suggest more metaphors to describe the strange trees that the Tin Woodman had to battle.

ASK YOURSELF:

1. What do the trees and/or branches remind me of?

_____

2. How are the trees and the item I named alike in appearance?

_____

3. How are they alike in function?

_____

4. From what source did each come? Are the sources alike?

_____

Write your metaphorical statement about the trees here.

_____

_____

_____

MNEMONICS

Memory strategies that assist
in recalling data.

ACRONYMS

Short words that help to remember a
sequence of items (NASA, OSHA, U.S.A.).

THE LOCI TECHNIQUE

Visualizing a path and specific landmarks
along that path. The landmark represents
data.

PAIRED ASSOCIATION

Connecting two or more unrelated items
with a visual image.

EXAGGERATION

Increasing the size of the object(s) to be
remembered.

MNEMONICS

Some acronyms are mnemonics to help remember the names of organizations.

For example: Fairy tale witches might belong to

S. P. E. L. L.

which stands for: **S**cientifically **P**erfect **E**nchantments **L**acking **L**ove

What night be the name of the organization for each of the letters that follow?

1. The seven dwarfs belong to the miner's union M.I.N.E.

_____

2. Elves belong to a little people's organization S.M.A.L.L.

_____

3. Fairies belong to W.A.N.D.

_____

4. Railroad men, like John Henry and Casey Jones, belong to P.U.S.H.

_____

5. The Wizard of Oz belongs to the Wizard's Union F.A.K.E.

_____

6. Paul Bunyan and other lumber men belong to L.O.G.

_____

MNEMONICS

Here is a story to help one remember the names of the Rocky Mountain States.

A TALL-TALE CHARACTER

Cool Ike, a tall-tale character, was just about the best guide the Rocky Mountains had ever known. Folks came from all over the world to be led by Ike across Colorado's Continental Divide, explore a Crystal Ice Cave in Idaho, or go birdwatching for the Mountain Bluebirds of Nevada. Nobody could remember a time when Cool Ike hadn't been around. Folks in Wyoming swore that Cool Ike was older than Old Faithful. Year after year he led folks through the Big Sky country of Montana and across Utah's Rainbow Bridge. Cool Ike was so popular that his hiking tours were booked up months in advance. He liked to brag that he had never lost a hiker.

A trip with Cool Ike was something to remember. Hikers would trail behind the spritely old man, wiping sweat from their brows as they climbed higher and higher. One thing folks noticed about Cool Ike was that no matter how high or how far he climbed, he never wiped a single bead of sweat from his brow. Even more surprising, when the hikers stopped to drink from their canteens, Cool Ike never took a sip of water. "Amazing!" they all said. "It's hotter than spit on a griddle. How can that old man move so fast and climb so high without breaking a sweat and needing a drink of water?"

Ike never told anyone his secret. Being a mountain man, he never went to the city. So when his underwear got holes, he didn't bother to sew them up. The mountain breezes could just flow right through. That was how Ike kept cool because

C-ool   I-ke   N-ever   W-ore   M-ended   U-nderwear.

C-COLORADO, I-IDAHO, N-NEVADA, W-WYOMING, M-MONTANA, U- UTAH

Create a story to help one remember the names of the Great Lakes using the mnemonic: **HOMES**.

H-uron, **O**-ntario, **M**-ichigan, **E**-rie, **S**-uperior

102

ORIGINALITY

The ability to generate novel, non-traditional, or unexpected ideas.

1. Determine and define the situation.

2. Define what is to be accomplished.

3. Brainstorm for original or unique ideas.

4. Interpret the ideas in clever, unique ways.

ORIGINALITY

The Maid on the Glass Mountain
from *East O' the Sun and West O' the Moon*
by Peter Asbjornsen
Putnam's, 1908

It is midnight on St. John's night and Cinderlad is crouched in the hayloft waiting to see what strange creature comes on this special night each year to eat all of the grass in the meadow. The two previous years his brothers had been sent to watch but were so frightened by the clatter and the noise that they ran away. A rumble in the distance grew louder and louder. The hayloft shook and Cinderlad was thrown to the floor. Picking himself up, he marched outside to see a huge, gleaming horse with the copper armor of a knight on the ground beside it. Cinderlad jumped on the horse and rode it to a hiding place and then went home to his family. For three years in a row, Cinderlad kept watch on the special night, and each year he found a horse larger and grander than the last.

Now, in this same country there was a king who would give his daughter in marriage to any man who could ride up a mountain of glass and take three golden apples from her lap. The knights came from far and wide, and even Cinderlad's brothers came, but no one could ride up the mountain. Finally one last knight rode up to the base of the mountain. He was on a large, grand horse and wore a suit of copper. Who do you suppose he is? And will he win the hand of the princess? To find out, read *The Maid on the Glass Mountain.*

When Cinderlad saw the huge prancing horse eating all of the grass in the field, he knew he had to put a stop to it. He also wanted to capture and keep the horse. But the horse was bigger than any he had ever seen and looked quite fierce. Cinderlad was only a very small boy.

He looked in his backpack and pulled out:

a rope	a spoon
a rock	a candle
a bottle	a glass
a blanket	

Work with a partner or small group. Decide how Cinderlad would use any or all of the items in his backpack in an original way to capture the horse.

ORIGINALITY

"Weather" or Not!

You are the owner of an employment agency. Mrs. Snow, Mr. Frost, Queen Wind, and King Hail, who are all unemployed now, have just walked into your office. The weather report in the giant's garden looks extremely bad for their futures since King Spring has taken over. They have come to the employment agency for help before it is too late! You need to come up with an original idea for a rich and prosperous future for one of them. First you must decide whom you wish to work with. List that person below and give at least two reasons explaining why you chose that person.

Name: _____

Reasons: _____

_____

Design a new and bright future for the client chosen. Include the following information:

Type of work: _____

Place to live: _____

Financial status: _____

New friends: _____

Recreational activities: _____

And any other important aspects that will affect your client's new life style:

_____

_____

_____

You will be paid a percentage of your client's future income, so do the best you can.

For a story about a giant's garden, read *The Selfish Giant* by Oscar Wilde.

PERCEPTUAL THINKING

The ability to examine an object, event, or situation by stretching the mind to perceive beyond established patterns.

FOR EVENTS OR SITUATIONS

Look at the positive

Look at the negative

Look at the interesting

Look at the irrelevant

Look at the consequences

Look at the antecedents

Look at the dominant idea

FOR OBJECTS

Look closely

Think about what you are seeing

Don't overlook the obvious

Look for relationships

PERCEPTUAL THINKING

THINKING ABOUT KINGS AND QUEENS

List the positive things about being a king.

List the negative things about being a king.

List the interesting things about being a king.

List qualities irrelevant to being a king.

What is the dominant feature of kinghood?

List the positive things about being a queen.

List the negative things about being a queen.

List the interesting things about being a queen.

List qualities irrelevant to being a queen.

What is the dominant feature of queenhood?

After looking at the answers you listed above, would you like to be a king or a queen? Why or why not?

107

PERCEPTUAL THINKING

PERCEPTION EQUALS VALUE EQUALS ACTION

Name different characters from fairy tales or fantasies who would agree with with the statements below. What action of the character leads you to believe that he or she would agree with the statement?

Example:

1. **Facts are more important than fantasy.**

   Klaus from *A Series of Unfortunate Events*.

   Klaus was a great reader of non-fiction and valued books more than anything else. His first reaction when his house burned down was that the library (and his books) had been destroyed.

2. **A thing is real only if you can see it, hear it, touch it, or taste it.**

   _____

   _____

   _____

3. **Economic welfare is more important than beauty.**

   _____

   _____

   _____

4. **The world exists so that humans can do with it whatever they wish.**

   _____

   _____

   _____

5. **Nothing is to be believed without proof.**

   _____

   _____

   _____

6. **Happiness is the result of getting exactly what you want, when you want it.**

   _____

   _____

   _____

PLANNING

Organizing a method for achieving a specific solution or outcome.

1. Goal identification: State the problem or project.

2. List and locate necessary materials.

3. List steps necessary to complete the project.

4. Identify problems.

5. Follow planning steps.

PLANNING

The Old Woman and the Red Pumpkin,
translated by Betsy Bang.
Illustrated by Molly Bang.
Macmillan, 1975.

A bear and a tiger saw a huge red pumpkin rolling along and singing. They gave it a push and followed curiously behind it, until a jackal joined them. "What's a pumpkin doing singing?" the Jackal said. He took a stick, broke open the pumpkin, and out popped the very same little old lady the animals had been planning to eat. But the clever old lady, who had outwitted them once before, knew just how to do it again.

Develop a plan for the old lady to help her escape from the animals.

1. What needs to be done? _____

_____

2. What materials will she need? _____

_____

3. Will she need help from others? Who? _____

_____

4. What problems may arise and how will she cope with them?

Problem	Solution
_____	_____
_____	_____
_____	_____

5. What steps will she take?

   A. _____

   B. _____

   C. _____

   D. _____

   E. _____

110

PLANNING EXERCISE

INDICTMENT: The People against Hansel and Gretel, accused of breaking and entering, robbery, and the murder of a senior citizen who lived in the Gingerbread House.

INDICTMENT: The People against Jack, who knowingly trespassed into the Giant's yard and stole the Giant's hen and harp.

INDICTMENT: The People against the Queen, who deliberately broke her contract with Rumplestiltskin, refusing to give up her child as promised.

INDICTMENT: For fraud against the members of the Town Council of Hamelin, who verbally contracted the services of one Pied Piper while having no intention of living up to the terms of payment in the contract.

Your group is to plan the prosecution for one of the above charges, or the defense against one of the above charges.

CONSIDER

RESOURCES NEEDED:

Authorities you need to consult

Sources of additional information

Witnesses to call

STEPS

How will you present the case?

What will you bring up first? Second?

In what order will witnesses be called? Why?

PROBLEMS

List problems you might have.

What negative points might the opposition bring up?

What problems might you foresee in jury selection?

What is your strategy for dealing with each forseeable problem?

PREDICTING

To forecast or anticipate, based on evidence, what might happen.

1. Clarify what is to be predicted.

2. Analyze data to find a basis for predicting.

3. Make a tentative prediction.

4. Consider related data and modify predictions as necessary.

Read the following story aloud. Stop after each question in the story and ask students for predictions. Check to see that the student has a reason for the student's prediction.

The Contented Old Woman

An old tale adapted by Nancy Polette

One day a poor old woman was digging potatoes in her garden. All at once she stooped and pulled out of the earth a big iron pot full of gold. She was as pleased as she could be.

She dragged it a little way toward her house, and looked again to make sure that it was full of gold. What do you think she found?

The gold had turned into silver! She was as pleased as she could be. She dragged it a little further and had to stop for breath. She looked again to make sure it was full of silver. What do you suppose had happened?

The silver had turned to copper pennies. Still she was as pleased as she could be. At the door she looked again to make sure that she had her pennies safe. Well, what do you think she saw?

There was nothing in the pot but a heavy stone. She remembered that she needed just such a stone to keep her door open. She was still as pleased as she could be. As she stooped to pick up the stone, what do you suppose happened?

The stone turned into a hideous dragon breathing fire. He jumped over her flower beds and flew away. Do you think the old woman was cross then?

No, she clapped her hands and cried, "Oh, how lucky I am! He might have eaten me up, house and garden and all!" So the contented old woman baked potatoes for supper and went to sleep in her cozy bed.

PREDICTIVE READING

Predictive questions to ask

Ask about what *will* be read, not what *has been* read.

1. What does the title mean?

2. What will the story be about?

3. What is the problem?

4. What will happen next?

5. Why do you predict that?

6. What are other possibilities?

7. Given what you know, what do you think will be the outcome?

8. How can we find out?

9. When were you sure?

10. What is this story really about (what is the theme)?

PREDICTING ACTION IN A STORY

In the story of *The Whipping Boy* by Sid Flieschman, Prince Brat refuses to learn to read or write. The outlaws insist that he send a note to his father, the king, demanding ransom.

Suppose that Prince Brat simply wanted his father to know he is safe and also wants to tell his father of his travels. He might purchase a ready-made letter like the one below; have someone read it to him and check the boxes that will best tell of his adventures.

BEFORE READING THE STORY, check the boxes you think Prince Brat might choose.

Dear Father:

1. I ran away to:
   a. __ avoid a whipping
   b. __ relieve boredom
   c. __ join the circus

2. I was captured by:
   a. __ a smelly robber
   b. __ a two-headed dragon
   c. __ a girl with a pet bear

3. I escaped by:
   a. __ becoming invisible
   b. __ changing myself into a cat
   c. __ running away

4. I was surprised to learn that the people of our kingdom:
   a. __ want a new king
   b. __ thought that the whipping boy had kidnapped me
   c. __ call me Prince Brat

5. To escape further danger I hid in:
   a. __ an underground cave
   b. __ a sewer full of rats
   c. __ an apple barrel

6. During my travels I learned a lot about:
   a. __ rats and rat fights
   b. __ trusting others
   c. __ myself

Answers: 1. B, 2. A, 3. C, 4. C, 5. B, 6. C

PROBLEM SOLVING

1. Identify and define the problem.

2. List important facts about the problem or situation.

3. List alternative solutions to the problem.

4. List criteria for appraising each solution.

5. Evaluate each solution, giving a numerical value to each. A value of 1 is low, and a value of 5 is high. Repeat using several criteria.

6. Total the values for each alternative solution.

7. State the best solution(s).

8. Devise a plan to gain acceptance of the solution by others.

A PROBLEM-SOLVING MODEL

Every story has a problem that must be solved. Read a story to the point where the problem arises. *Before* finishing the story to see how the author solves the problem, try solving the problem yourself by using the steps listed below. Then finish the story. Did you like your solution better? The author's? Were they the same?

Title _____

Author _____

1. What important facts can you state about the situation?

    _____

    _____

    _____

2. State the major problem.

    _____

    _____

3. List as many ways to deal with the problem as you can. These are your alternatives.

    _____

    _____

    _____

4. Select the three best ideas and enter them on the decision grid below.

5. Two criteria for judging ideas are provided in the grid. Add a third criterion of your own.

6. Evaluate each idea on a scale of one to five. A rating of one is poor; a rating of five is excellent.

Scale 1–5 Best Ideas	Is It Fast?	Is It Low-Cost?	Your criterion: _____

PROBLEM SOLVING

The Funny Little Woman
by Arlene Mosel, E. P. Dutton, 1972.

THE GREAT RICE DUMPLING BAKE-OFF

For the first time in Japan, a Great Rice Dumpling Bake-Off was to be held. The Funny Little Woman was chosen as one of the finalists to participate in the bake-off in Tokyo next week. However, she is still trapped in the Oni kitchen and is guarded day and night by two of the Oni. You must take action to enable her to participate in the bake-off. Completing this page will help you decide what action to take.

I.   State the problem.

_____

_____

II. List three good ways to deal with the problem. List the most probable result of each action. Star your first choice.

   A. _____

   Result: _____

   B. _____

   Result: _____

   C. _____

   Result: _____

Congratulations! Your plan works and the Funny Little Woman won the bake-off!

III. Describe her prize here. (It is not money.)

_____

_____

_____

118

PROBLEM SOLVING

FAIRY TALE PROBLEMS TO SOLVE

Define the problem. Set up the problem-solving grid. (See an example on the previous page.) List possible solutions to the problem. Develop criteria for judging each solution using a numerical value: 1 = no, 2 = maybe, 3 = yes.

The solution with the highest score is the one to try.

1. The hero or heroine must discover why the shoes of twelve princesses are worn out every night even when the princesses are locked securely in their rooms each evening.

2. The hero or heroine arrives at a house with no children, for every newborn child is spirited away by a giant hand that comes down the chimney.

3. The hero or heroine keeps watch in a chapel near the coffin of a beautiful princess, who nightly rises to slay any brave enough to guard her.

4. A hero or heroine enters a land in mourning. Its prince has been captured by ugly trolls who keep him in an enchanted sleep in a dark cave. The king offers half his kingdom to anyone who can find and rescue the missing prince.

5. A dreadful and dangerous monster dwells in the dungeon of the king's palace. The king refuses permission for the princess to marry her childhood sweetheart unless he first overcomes the monster.

6. A little girl, twelve years old, is shut up in a tower thirty feet in height, with sides as slick as glass all around. There were no stairs or doors, but at the top of the tower is a small window. The little girl wants to escape.

QUESTIONING: HIGHER-ORDER

ANALYSIS

Differentiate fact from opinion.
What assumptions are necessary for_____ to be true?
What is the fallacy in _____?
Is there enough information to support_____?
What distinguishes _____ from _____?
Examine _____ and _____ for similarities.
Examine _____ and _____ for differences.
Debate the idea that _____.
How would you test/communicate/clarify/infer/identify a problem or solution?

SYNTHESIS

Propose a solution to_____.
Organize a plan to _____.
Use the technique of _____ to _____.
Come up with a theory that would account for_____.
If _____is true, what else might be true?
Modify _____ so that _____.
Devise a _____. Write a _____.

EVALUATION

Critique your work. Is _____ correct?
How do you feel about _____ as opposed to
_____?
Are the conclusions supported by the evidence?
Which course of action would be best? Why?
Given the situation, what decision would you make? Why?

MORE HIGHER-ORDER QUESTIONS

A. Drawing logical conclusions
   Students deduce conclusions based upon evidence in text.
   - The ___ is/will probably ___ because ___.
   - Which word best describes ___?

B. Making generalizations
   Students use inductive reasoning to form generalizations.
   - You can tell from this passage that ___.
   - The author of this passage gives you reason to believe that ___

C. Evaluating and making judgements
   Students make judgements based on evidence from text.
   - Which best describes ___?
   - The author provides evidence that ___.

D. Recognizing author's point of view
   Students infer author's attitude or opinion from information in the passage.
   - The author probably wrote this passage in order to ___.
   - You can tell from the story that the author views ___ with ___.

E. Recognizing persuasive devices
   Students will recognize persuasive language, stereotypes, fallacy in an argument, and evidence of bias.
   - When the author said ___, she was trying to convince the reader that ___.
   - The author used the phrase "___" to try to convince you that ___.
   - The author tries to convince the reader of ___ by ___.

REVERSIBLE THINKING

The ability to think back though an operation from the end to the beginning.

1. Read or tell a fairy tale or a situation that involves sequential steps.

2. Retell the events of the tale or the steps in the situation in reverse order.

EXAMPLES

Tell the tale of Red Riding Hood from the end to the beginning.

Think about an apple pie. Where did it come from? Retrace the steps from pie to apple.

REVERSIBLE THINKING: THE CIRCLE STORY

Here is a reversible story. It ends at the same place it begins.

There was once a princess who was never satisfied. She always wanted to be where she was not. One day she said to her fairy godmother, "I am tired of this old palace. Take me to the village. I want to meet the people." The princess was taken to the village, but no one would talk to her. The people bowed in awe of her. The princess said to her fairy godmother, "This village is very unfriendly. Take me to the Enchanted Forest." The princess found herself in the Enchanted Forest. It was dark. It was damp. It was filled with wild animals that made terrible sounds. "I do not like this at all," the princess cried. "Take me to the seaside where the fisherman and his wife live." The princess found herself at the seaside. The waves looked dark and angry. The salt water sprayed her face. "The seaside is dark and wet," the princess exclaimed. "I do not like it at all. Take me back to my palace." The princess got her wish. Her loving parents welcomed her. The only beast was her pet mockingbird. Her servants drew her a lovely warm bubble bath and the princess decided there was no place like home after all!

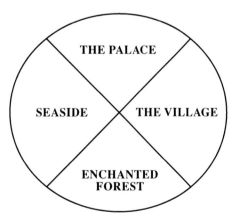

MORE CIRCLE STORIES

The Stonecutter by Gerald McDermott, Penguin, New York, 1975.

One Fine Day by Nonny Hogrogian, Macmillan, New York, 1971.

Try creating your own circle story!

SEQUENCING

1. Choose items or events to be sequenced.

2. Consider the relationship between the items or events.

3. Order the events or items according to an ascendng or descending relationship.

   Size: from small to large, or large to small.

   Value: from less to more, or more to less.

   Time: From now to later, or later to now.

   Position: from near to far, or far to near.

   Alphabetical: from A to Z, or Z to A.

   Events: from first to last, or last to first.

SEQUENCING EVENTS

Puss in Boots
by Charles Perrault, Fairy Tales, 1697.

Modern picture book versions include:

Puss in Boots, illustrated by Lorinda Bryan Cauley, Harcourt, 1986.

Puss in Boots, illustrated by Fred Marcellino, Farrar, 1990.

BOOKTALK

When the miller died, his oldest son received the mill, his middle son received a donkey, and his youngest son received a cat. The youngest son had no idea how to make a living with the cat except to kill it and eat it and make a hat of its fur. The cat, hearing this, promised that if the boy would give him boots and a sack that he would make the young man wealthy. Using the sack the cat manages to catch rabbits and partridges and take them to the king from his master, the "Marquis of Carabas." When the king and his party are out riding one morning, the cat tells the boy to take off his clothes and jump into the river. As the coach passes by the cat calls to the king to save his master who has been robbed and is in danger of drowning. The boy is rescued and falls in love with the king's daughter. But how can he convince the king that he is worthy of her? Leave it to Puss in Boots to solve the problem!

Directions: Cut the strips apart. Give a set of strips to a small group of three or four students. Students work together to put the strips in correct order to tell the story. Then students work together to add correct capitalization and punctuation. When a group has completed its task, a monitor or teacher can check for correctness.

long long ago a miller died and left his
youngest son a cat who promised to make the
young man wealthy the cat caught rabbits and gave them
to the king from his master then the boy pretended
to drown and the kings men saved him and took him to
the palace where the boy fell in love
with the kings daughter
but how can he convince the king he is worthy of her

STORY SEQUENCING

The Korean Cinderella
by Shirley Climo, HarperCollins, 1993.

Pear Blossom is as lovely as the pear tree planted in celebration of her birth, but she is mistreated by Omoni, her jealous stepmother. Omoni forces her to rise before the sun and cook and clean until midnight, and demands that Pear Blossom complete three tasks no human could possibly do alone. She is to fill a water jar with a hole in it the size of an onion, polish every grain of rice from a huge sack scattered all over the courtyard, and weed the rice paddies in less than a day. But Pear Blossom is not alone. With the help of three magical animals, Pear Blossom is able to attend the festival and becomes a nobleman's wife.

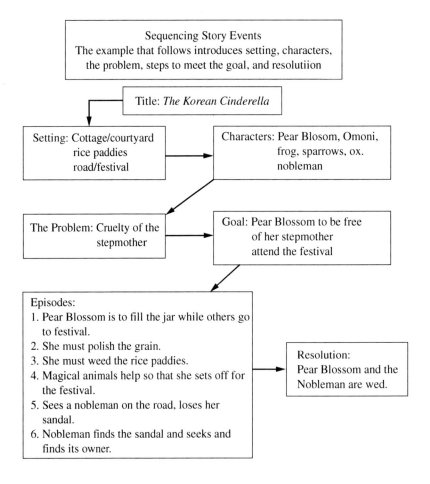

Sequencing Story Events
The example that follows introduces setting, characters, the problem, steps to meet the goal, and resolutiion

Title: *The Korean Cinderella*

Setting: Cottage/courtyard
rice paddies
road/festival

Characters: Pear Blosom, Omoni,
frog, sparrows, ox.
nobleman

The Problem: Cruelty of the
stepmother

Goal: Pear Blossom to be free
of her stepmother
attend the festival

Episodes:
1. Pear Blossom is to fill the jar while others go to festival.
2. She must polish the grain.
3. She must weed the rice paddies.
4. Magical animals help so that she sets off for the festival.
5. Sees a nobleman on the road, loses her sandal.
6. Nobleman finds the sandal and seeks and finds its owner.

Resolution:
Pear Blossom and the
Nobleman are wed.

Sequencing with the Story Map

Make a map of the Story by Filling In the Boxes

Characters	Setting

Problem

Events

1.
2.
3.
4.
5.

Solution

SYMBOLIC THINKING

1. Discover a relationship between two events, items, persons, or ideas.

2. Develop a list of objects or illustrations which represent the relationship.

3. Design a symbol to show the relationship.

In the fairy tale *Many Moons* by James Thurber (Harcourt, 1943), Princess Lenore wanted the moon.

What symbols for the moon might the court jester have given her?

SYMBOLIC THINKING

The Tongue-Cut Sparrow

Retold in verse by Nancy Polette

A mean old woman took a tiny bird,
And cut its tongue so it couldn't be heard.
The bird flew away and the neighbors gave chase,
And followed the bird to a tree-filled place.

They were welcomed and fed and before they could ask it,
Were given a marvelous, magical basket.

The mean old woman, she wanted one, too.
So went to find the bird to see what it would do.
"Give me jewels," she said, "and a fancy dress."
Did the bird give her jewels? What would you guess?

Now the neighbors were gentle and kind and needy,
But the cranky old woman was mean and greedy.
So her gift wasn't silver or jewels or gold
But a basket of troubles—now the story's told.

1. How is the basket related to the villagers?

2. How is the basket related to the old woman?

3. What does the basket symbolize?

4. What does the bird symbolize?

Design a symbol to show the meaning of this story.

SYMBOLS AND SIGNS

A symbol is a very simple picture that can communicate important information without using words.

Here are symbols that might be needed in fairy tale land.

Draw a symbol to represent each idea.

The first one is done for you.

FISHING ALLOWED

BEWARE OF THE WITCH

ENCHANTED FOREST

NO MONSTERS ALLOWED

MAGIC SHOP

130

Write Your Own Fairy Tale

What makes a good writer? It is the ability to **think** of new ideas and new ways of saying things. Writers also have the ability **to see** things in great detail in order that they can create on paper vivid scenes for the reader.

Seeing detail and **thinking of new ideas** are things that do not just happen. Both of these things take PRACTICE! When you visit a new place, practice making a list of fifty things you see. Do this same thing in a familiar place. You will be surprised at the many things you have not noticed before.

Original ideas can come to you if you EXERCISE YOUR MIND (so that you don't tell only stories you have heard or stories everyone else has heard). Just as athletes warm up their bodies before the big game, you must warm up your mind before you start to write. Think of MANY MANY ways for your characters to solve their problems. Then choose your BEST IDEA—not necessarily your first idea.

Here are some MIND EXERCISES for you to do before you begin writing your own fairy tale.

1. Name ten things a dragon can do other than breathe fire and roar.
2. Give five reasons why the reader should feel sorry for Snow White's wicked stepmother.
3. Think of arguments a prosecutor might use in putting Hansel and Gretel on trial for murder.
4. Name ten things you might find in a throne room other than a throne.
5. Give as many ways as you can to punish the evil character in a fairy tale without causing physical harm.

LITTLE NO-ACCOUNT

The Story Begins

A woman had three daughters. The oldest had only one eye in the middle of her forehead. The second had three eyes, one also in the middle of her forehead. The youngest, however, had two eyes like other people.

"You with your two eyes are no better than anybody else. You do not belong to us," her mother said. So they knocked her about, gave her shabby clothes and food which was left over from their own meals, and called her Little No-Account. The tasks she was given to do would have been enough for six servants.

List the tasks Little No-Account had to do each day. The last task is listed for you.

(1) _____

_____

_____

_____

_____

_____

_____

She had to go out into the fields and look after the goat.

_____

Little No-Account was always hungry, and on this day she sat down on a hillock and began to cry. Then a woman s voice said, "Little No-Account, why do you cry?" She told the woman of her cruel treatment, her shabby clothes, and her hunger.

The wise woman said, "Only say these words to your goat and a neatly laid table will stand before you. When you have eaten enough, repeat the words and the table will disappear."

Then, faster than the blink of an eye, the wise woman vanished.

Write the magic words that Little No-Account must say.

(2) _____

_____

_____

Scarcely had she uttered the words when there stood before her a magnificently laid table.

Describe what was on the table.

(3) _____

_____

_____

_____

_____

_____

Little No-Account ate until she was full. Then she again uttered the magic words and the table disappeared.

For the next few evenings when she came home with the goat, she did not touch the food scraps that were left for her.

Middle Three Eyes said, "Little No-Account is leaving her food and she used to eat everything. I will go with her to the meadow tomorrow and see what she does there."

But Little No-Account saw what Middle Three Eyes had in mind and she thought of a way to keep her from discovering the secret of the goat.

Tell what happens when they get into the meadow. What is Little No-Account's plan? Tell also how the plan does not work and how Middle Three Eyes discovers the secret. The last part of your story should read: That is how Middle Three Eyes discovered the secret of the goat.

(4) _____

_____

_____

_____

_____

_____

_____

_____

_____

_____

_____

_____

_____

_____

_____

That is how Middle Three Eyes discovered the secret of the goat.

_____

When the envious mother heard the tale from Middle Three Eyes, she fetched a butcher's knife and struck it into the goat's heart so that it fell down dead.

When Little No-Account saw this, she went out full of grief, seated herself on the hillock, and wept bitter tears. When she looked up, the wise woman again stood before her and was told what had happened.

The wise woman said, "Here is some good advice. Beg your sisters to give you the heart of the goat. Bury it in the ground before the house door and it will turn out lucky for you."

This Little No-Account did. The next morning when the sisters awoke and went to the house door together, there stood a most wonderful, splendid tree, its branches loaded with unbelievable treasures!

Describe this tree. Place on its branches a most wonderful treasure. Try to think of something very unusual.

(5) _____

_____

_____

_____

_____

_____

_____

The two greedy sisters pushed Little No-Account to the ground and ran toward the wonderful tree. Each wanted to be first to gather the treasure from its branches.

But when they reached to tree, not a single treasure could they gather.

Tell what the tree does to prevent the sisters from gathering the treasure.

(6) _____

_____

_____

_____

_____

_____

_____

Then Little No-Account said, "Let me try. Perhaps I will prosper better."

"You!" cried the mother, "With your two eyes, what can you do?"

Tell how Little No-Account is able to pluck the treasure from the tree's branches. The last line of this part of your story should read: But her mother and sisters were envious because she alone could get the treasure and they behaved still more cruelly to her.

(7) _____

_____

_____

_____

_____

_____

_____

_____

_____

_____

_____

But her mother and sisters were envious because she alone could get the treasure and they behaved still more cruelly to her. _____

_____

It happened as they stood together by the tree one day that a young Prince came by. Little No-Account was sent to the house so that he would not see her.

"To whom does this wonderful tree belong?" the Prince asked. "She who gives me a treasure from it shall have whatever she wishes."

Once again the selfish sisters tried to gather the treasure from the branches. This time, however, the Prince was watching and saw that they could not do so.

"It is a puzzle that the tree belongs to you and yet you have not the power of gathering anything from it," he said.

Then the sisters admitted that there was indeed a third sister, who might not show herself because she had only two eyes like other people. Just then the Prince saw Little No-Account at the cottage window.

Tell what the Prince does now. What does he say? How does Little No-Account respond? End this part of the story with the words: She handed the treasure to the Prince.

(8) _____

_____

_____

_____

_____

_____

_____

She handed the treasure to the Prince._____

As he accepted the treasure, the Prince saw the girl's work-worn hands and shabby clothes and guessed at the cruel way in which she was treated.

"Little No-Account," he said, "I have the power to grant you a single wish. Name whatever you wish and your heart's desire shall be yours."

Now you must have Little No-Account think what her wish will be. List at least five things she might consider and give the reasons for the one thing she finally chooses. The last line of this part of your story should read: The cruel mother and sisters were left alone with the tree.

(9) _____

_____

_____

_____

_____

_____

_____

_____

_____

The cruel mother and sisters were left alone with the tree.

_____

"The wonderful tree remains with us," they said, "Even though we cannot gather the treasure from it, everyone will stand before it, come up to us, and praise us."

But the next morning ...

Tell what happens the next morning to the tree and to the mother and sisters. Also tell how Little No-Account spent the rest of her life. Did she marry the Prince? If not, what did she do? Think of an unusual ending for your story, one that will surprise your reader!

(10) _____

_____

_____

_____

_____

_____

_____

_____

_____

THE TOWER OF THE DRAGON

With details and problem solutions by

_____

Chapter One

Once upon a time there was a king who had three sons and a daughter. He kept the daughter in a cage and guarded her as carefully as the eyes in his head. When she was grown she begged her father one evening to let her go out and take a walk before the castle with her brothers. The father consented, but hardly was she out the door when a dragon came swooping down out of the sky.

Write your description here of the most terrible dragon you can imagine.

_____

_____

_____

_____

_____

_____

_____

_____

This terrible dragon seized the maiden and carried her away deep into the forest before her brothers could as much as offer a shout in her defense.

They rushed headlong back to the king, told him of their misfortune, and begged permission to go and seek their stolen sister.

The father consented and gave each of them a horse and everything needed for the journey. Each brother carried with him a trusty bow and arrow, a rope, and a bag of food.

Chapter Two

After many wanderings the brothers came upon a tower which stood neither upon earth or in heaven. The dragon droppings at the tower's base told them that this was indeed the place where their sister was held captive. There was no door at the foot of the tower. At the top, three hundred feet into the sky, only one small window could be seen. The brothers at once began to take counsel among themselves as to how they could reach it.

Describe your plan for gaining entrance to the tower. The brothers can use only those items they have taken with them. End your plan with the words: and the youngest brother was chosen to carry out the plan.

_____

_____

_____

_____

_____

_____

_____

_____

and the youngest brother was chosen to carry out the plan._____

_____

Chapter Three

Arriving at the tower he went from room to room, until at last he came to one where he saw his sister sitting, with the Dragon's head in her lap. The Dragon was fast asleep. When the sister saw her brother, she was greatly frightened and begged him to flee before the dragon should awake. This he would not do, but struck out boldly and dealt the dragon a heavy blow on the head. The Dragon, without awakening put his hand up to the spot, murmuring, "something hit me right here." A second and a third blow brought the same response.

"Blows won't kill the Dragon," the sister whispered in her brother's ear. "But I have a plan which will do away with him forever. Listen well, dear brother, I shall tell you just what to do."

Tell what the sister's plan is and describe just what the youngest brother must do to carry out the plan. The last line of this part of your story should read: Then the Princess flew into her brother's arms and smothered him with kisses. The evil dragon was dead!

_____

_____

_____

_____

_____

_____

_____

_____

_____

_____

Then the Princess flew into her brother s arms and smothered him

with kisses. The evil dragon was dead!

Chapter Four

After this, she took him by the hand and began to lead him through all the rooms of the tower. First she led him into a room where a white horse with wings and a harness of pure gold stood before a manger.

"Now," the Princess said, "you must meet the other maidens the Dragon has captured and imprisoned in this tower. He stole each away from her family because of her beauty and her very special treasure."

The sister led her brother into a chamber where the first beautiful maiden sat.

Describe the room and the maiden and tell what her special treasure is.

_____

_____

_____

_____

_____

_____

_____

_____

_____

_____

From this room she led him into a chamber where another maiden was.

Describe this maiden, her room, and her treasure. Make your description as unusual as possible.

_____

_____

_____

_____

_____

_____

_____

_____

_____

Last, the sister led her brother into a room where a third maiden, a simple farm girl, was stringing pearls. At her feet a golden hen, with a brood of chicks, was picking up pearls from a golden basin.

Chapter Five

The Princess and her brother then went back into the room where the dead Dragon lay, dragged him out and threw him head-foremost down to the earth. When the other brothers saw him they were filled with terror. But the younger brother called to them from the tower window, "Come, help me get the maidens down safely from the tower."

Describe how the brother will get the maidens safely to earth with their treasures. The last line of this part of your story should read: In this way the maidens were safely delivered to the earth. Only the youngest brother now remained in the tower.

_____

_____

_____

_____

_____

_____

_____

_____

_____

In this way the maidens were safely delivered to the earth. Only the youngest brother now remained in the tower.

_____

Chapter Six

But now, sad though it is to tell, it is a fact that the two older brothers were filled with envy because youngest brother was the hero who had discovered all these things and rescued their sister from the tower. They looked at younger brother high up in the tower window and decided to leave him there. "We must make sure," said the eldest brother, "that he has no means of escape."

"Never fear," said middle brother, "We shall make sure he remains where he is."

Even though their sister, the Princess, protested, they warned her they would return and kill this youngest brother if she breathed a word of their scheme to their father or anyone else. Thus, she and the other maidens held their silence.

Tell what the brothers do to make it impossible for youngest brother to leave the tower. Remember that they must leave him alive. The last line of this account should read: Then they rode away, taking the younger brother's horse with them.

_____

_____

_____

_____

_____

_____

_____

_____

_____

_____

_____

Then they rode away, taking the younger brother's horse with them.

_____

Chapter Seven

On their way back to the castle, they came upon a shepherd boy with his sheep. They dressed him like their brother and brought him home to their father, once again reminding their sister and the maidens, with fearful threats, not under any circumstances to reveal the secret.

After a time, word came to the youngest brother in the tower that his brothers and the shepherd were about to marry the three maidens. His thoughts went again to the lovely farm maiden. He wanted her for his wife.

"I must escape," he said to the winged horse. "Why is it that you cannot fly? It must be that you are under a spell. If only I knew the secret words to release you, we could take flight together!" Suddenly ...

Tell how youngest brother discovers the hiding place of the words which will break the spell and allow the winged horse to fly. Write the words (as a poem) that will break the spell.

May be copied for classroom use. *Teaching Skills with Fairy Tales and Fantasy*, by Nancy Polette
(Westport, CT: Teacher Ideas Press, an imprint of Libraries Unlimited). © 2005.

Chapter Eight

On the day appointed for the wedding, the youngest brother mounted the winged horse and flew down into the midst of the wedding guests as they were entering the church. He struck his brothers and the shepherd lightly on the back with his club, causing them to fall from their horses.

In a trice the Prince was surrounded by the wedding guests, who were determined that he should not escape. His eyes sought out the beautiful farm maiden, and when he found her, he took her hand and led her to the topmost step of the church where he turned and spoke to the now-silent crowd.

Write the Prince's speech here. How can he convince the crowd of his identity?

_____

_____

_____

_____

_____

_____

_____

_____

Chapter Nine

His sister and the maidens bore witness to the truth of his story, and when the King heard all this he was determined to punish the two elder brothers. "It must be a punishment to fit the crime!" the King declared.

Give an account here of the punishment the King decides on for the two older brothers. Remember, it must fit the crime.

_____

_____

_____

_____

_____

_____

_____

_____

_____

_____

_____

_____

_____

The young Prince and the farm maiden were married and the Prince was made heir to the throne. As for the other two maidens, one fell deeply in love with a Prince from another kingdom and became his wife. The other, so gentle and wise, was given a palace of her own. People came to her from all over the land, confident that her counsel would assist them in all times of trial and trouble.

BIBLIOGRAPHY

Asbjornsen, Peter. *East 'O the Sun and West 'O the Moon.* Putnam's, 1908.

Babbitt, Natalie. *Kneeknock Rise.* Farrar, 1984.

Bang, Betsy. *The Old Woman and the Red Pumpkin.* Illustrated by Molly Bang. Macmillan, 1975.

Baum, L. Frank. *The Wizard of Oz.* Illustrated by Michael Hague. Holt, 2000.

Cauley, Lorinda Bryan. *Puss in Boots.* Harcourt, 1986.

Climo, Shirley. *The Korean Cinderella.* HarperCollins, 1993.

Compton, Joanne. *Ashpet: An Appalachian Tale.* Illustrated by Ken Compton. Holiday House, 1994.

Czernecki, Stefan and Timothy Rhodes. *The Sleeping Bread.* Hyperion, 1992.

Dahl, Roald. *The BFG.* Illustrated by Quentin Blake. Farrar, 1982.

———. *Fantastic Mr. Fox.* Illustrated by Quentin Blake. Knopf, 1970.

———. *The Magic Finger.* Illustrated by Quentin Blake. Knopf, 1995.

———. *Matilda.* Illustrated by Quentin Blake. Viking, 1995.

———. *The Witches.* Johnathan Cape Publishers, 1983.

duBois, William Pene. *The Twenty One Balloons.* Viking, 1947.

Fleischman, Syd. *The Whipping Boy.* Illustrated by Peter Sis. Greenwillow, 1986.

Heide, Florence Parry. *The Shrinking of Treehorn.* Illustrated by Edward Gorey. Holiday House, 1971.

Hogrogian, Nonny. *One Fine Day.* Macmillan, 1971.

Hughes, Ted. *The Iron Giant.* Faber & Faber Ltd. 1995.

Isaacs, Anne. *Swamp Angel.* Illustrated by Paul O. Zelinsky. E. P. Dutton, 1994.

Jacques, Brian. *Redwall.* Philomel, 1986.

Johnson, Crockett. *Harold's Fairy Tale.* HarperCollins, 1956.

Lindgren, Astrid. *Pippi Longstocking.* Viking, 1950.

Mahy, Margaret. *The Seven Chinese Brothers.* Illustrated by Jean and Mou-sien Tseng. Scholastic, 1990.

Marcellino, Fred. *Puss in Boots.* Farrar, 1990.

McDermott, Gerald. *The Stonecutter.* Penguin, 1975.

Mosel, Arlene. *Tikki Tikki Tembo.* Illustrated by Blair Lent. Holt, 1968.

Park, Linda Sue. *A Single Shard.* Houghton Mifflin, 2002.

Paterson, Katherine. *Bridge to Terabithia.* Crowell, 1977.

Rawls, Wilson. *Where the Red Fern Grows.* Bantam, 2001.

Rowling, J. K. *Harry Potter and the Sorcerer's Stone.* Illustrated by Mary Grand-Pre. Scholastic, 1997.

Saint-Exupery, Antoine de. *The Little Prince.* Harcourt, 2000.

Selden, George. *The Cricket in Times Square.* Illustrated by Garth Williams. Farrar, 1960.

Snicket, Lemony. *The Reptile Room.* HarperCollins, 1999.

———. *The Wide Window.* HarperCollins, 2000.

Thurber, James. *Many Moons.* Harcourt, 1943.

Tolkein, J.R.R. *The Hobbit.* Illustrated by Michael Hauge. Houghton Mifflin, 1994.

Tolstoy, Alexi. *The Enormous Turnip.* Illustrated by Scott Goto. Harcourt, 2003.

Travers, Pamela. *Mary Poppins.* Illustrated by Mary Shepard. Harcourt, 1934.

Ungerer, Tomi. The *Three Robbers.* Atheneum, 1962.

Vaughan, Marcia. *Wombat Stew.* Silver Burdette, 1986.

Wagner, Jenny. *The Bunyip of Berkeley's Creek.* Bradbury, 1973.

White, E. B. *Charlotte's Web.* Illustrated by Garth Williams. HarperCollins, 1980.

INDEX

ABOUT THE AUTHOR

NANCY POLETTE is an educator with over 30 years experience. She has authored over 150 professional titles. She lives and works in O'Fallon, Missouri, where she is a professor at Lindenwood College.

CPSIA information can be obtained at www.ICGtesting.com
Printed in the USA
LVOW031958290212

271061LV00001B/3/P

9 781591 583202